ODYSSEY
OF YOUR SOUL

ODYSSEY
OF YOUR SOUL

A VOYAGE OF SELF-DISCOVERY

ELIZABETH CLARE PROPHET

SUMMIT UNIVERSITY PRESS®

Gardiner, Montana

ODYSSEY OF YOUR SOUL: A Voyage of Self-Discovery
by Elizabeth Clare Prophet
Copyright © 2011 Summit Publications, Inc.
All rights reserved

For information, contact Summit University Press,
63 Summit Way, Gardiner, MT 59030 USA.
Tel: 1-800-245-5445 or 406-848-9500
Website: www.SummitUniversityPress.com

Library of Congress Control Number 2011933111
ISBN 978-1-60988-025-5

SUMMIT UNIVERSITY 🌿 PRESS®
Summit University Press and 🌿 are trademarks registered in
the U.S. Patent and Trademark Office and in other countries.
All rights reserved

Cover and interior design by James Bennett Design
Credit: Cast of Odysseus from the Vatican, Shakko,
creativecommons.org/license/by-sa/3.01

Printed in the United States of America
15 14 13 12 11   1 2 3 4 5

This book is based on the lecture series "The Odyssey of Your Soul" by Elizabeth
Clare Prophet.

Notes and Disclaimers: (1) No guarantee is made by Summit University Press that
the practices described in this book will yield successful results for anyone at any time.
They are presented for informational purposes only, as the practice and proof of the
Science of Being rests with the individual. (2) Because gender-neutral language can
be cumbersome, we have often used *he* and *him* to refer to the individual. These terms
are not intended to exclude women or the feminine aspect of every person.

CONTENTS

Note on the Text of the *Odyssey*: Quotations are from three translations of the Greek text (Oxford University Press): Robert Fagles, Robert Fitzgerald, and Richmond Lattimore. Regardless of the translation used, the line numbers indicated are those of Lattimore. Spellings have been harmonized.

ILLUSTRATIONS

Homer, ancient Greek poet, being guided by Glaucus. Homer is traditionally regarded as author of the epics the Iliad and the Odyssey.

Introduction

A VOYAGE OF
SELF-DISCOVERY

FOLLOWING
THE ROUTE OF
ODYSSEUS

The Journey Begins

A VOYAGE OF SELF-DISCOVERY

Tales of the Trojan War and its heroes have fascinated kings and commoners alike for over three thousand years. For centuries, bards traveled far and wide reciting the epic adventures that began when Helen of Sparta was abducted by the Trojan prince Paris. Kings and warriors of the various Greek states set sail for Troy to force the return of Helen, "the face that launched a thousand ships." The war dragged on for ten years before the Greeks finally achieved their goal.

Around the eighth century BCE, the epic poems were set into written form. These are the literary masterpieces we know today as Homer's *Iliad* and *Odyssey*. The *Iliad* recounts the final year of the Trojan War. It speaks of glory and honor, key themes in ancient Greece. One of the *Iliad's* heroes is Odysseus, king of Ithaca. Once Odysseus commits to the battle, he is driven by a single purpose: The Greek campaign against Troy must succeed. Indeed, it is Odysseus who masterminds the Trojan Horse stratagem that brings victory to the Greeks.

Homer's *Odyssey* recounts the homeward journey of Odysseus following the fall of Troy. Singleness of purpose again drives Odysseus: He must reach Ithaca and restore order to his family, home and kingdom. What begins as a short voyage home from Troy turns into a heroic ten-year adventure that Odysseus survives only by drawing forth tremendous inner resources. After much hardship and many tests of character, some passed and others failed, Odysseus reaches home a changed man. The once shrewd, rash and arrogant king has become a wiser and more humble man.

THE STUFF HEROES ARE MADE OF

Odysseus is not the biggest and brawniest of the Greek heroes. He is, however, the most intelligent, and he is renowned as a master strategist. While Odysseus has his faults, he also has characteristics that are typical of a hero:

1. Odysseus keeps his eye on his goal.
2. He is not afraid to make a mistake.
3. He courageously accepts and faces his trials.
4. When he makes a mistake, he bounces back.
5. He learns from his mistakes.
6. He is not afraid of pain.
7. He endures.
8. He is open to discovering more about his inner self.

9. He does not dwell on the past.
10. He respects the gods.
11. He is obedient to their direction.
12. He has a mentor who intercedes for him.

FACETS OF BEING

Odysseus' character is complex, containing strengths and weaknesses. In this book his journey home is discussed as a series of trials in which his inner task is to transform the negative aspects of his character into their positive counterparts.

The brilliance of Homer's tale is that Odysseus' character can be seen to represent each one of us. Every episode offers insight into human nature. Underneath the intense battles and mythical encounters, the *Odyssey* can be read as an acknowledgment of the universal struggle to return home to our true self, to become whole, to be the hero or heroine we are meant to be. A symbolic reading of the *Odyssey* offers an understanding of why we so often know better but fail to do better. If we can understand and anchor the lessons of Odysseus' journey, we will better understand our own inner odyssey.

We all have within us the makings of a hero or heroine. We have all stumbled and we are all nonetheless worthy of finding our way home to a higher level of being. No matter what we have done in life, no matter how far we have fallen, no matter what shame or regret we carry within us, we also possess another side to our personality, a higher self, our true nature.

Our venture into the *Odyssey* offers both an understanding of the human condition and strategies for identifying and unshackling ourselves from the habitual character traits and attitudes that have held us back from reaching higher levels of our own being.

Like Odysseus, we are all multifaceted beings. We have traits that may include being adventurous, compassionate, courageous, determined, dutiful, enthusiastic, generous, humble, joyful, loyal, uplifting, and wise. We also have traits that may include being aggressive, careless, envious, insensitive, reckless, selfish, short-tempered, stubborn, and vengeful. The positive aspects are in constant battle with the negative aspects. Both seek to direct our journey, to grow stronger and dominate our personality.

The constant battle makes us weary. This is the suffering that Homer alludes to in the oracle's warning to Odysseus that if he goes to Troy he will not see his home again for twenty years. We suffer as we confront the darker traits within ourselves and seek to overcome them. Which side of our nature will win the battle? The one that we cultivate and nurture is the one that will win.

Where we direct our attention, our behaviors, and our thoughts determines what we will become. To change who we are requires a redirecting of this energy into new actions and thoughts. We all know that this is easier said than done. Think about all the New Year's resolutions that are broken before the end of January comes to pass. So many of us are determined to do things differently, but we fall back into old patterns and habits. We are determined to be kinder and more loving, to fulfill our obligations and to reach for our dreams, and still have time to smell the roses. But following through can be so difficult! This is the inner meaning behind Odysseus' long and arduous voyage of self-transformation. It is an internal battle to liberate his higher self.

THE CAST AND CREW

In Homer's tale, Odysseus has many companions on his journey. One hundred and forty-four men make up his crew. The Ithacans who fought under his command during the Trojan War now man the oars and set the sails in his ships. If we view the *Odyssey* as a symbolic story of an internal struggle taking place within Odysseus, then the crew members can be seen as representing the various facets of his personality. The giants, temptresses and monsters Odysseus meets along the way also symbolize parts of his own personality that he can no longer afford to ignore.

Many times during his journey, Odysseus defends his crew and praises them. On one level this can be seen as praise for that aspect of his character that the crew member represents. For example, Odysseus praises the *bravery* of a crew member who represents his own overly curious nature, but in reality that curiosity just leads to acting rashly. By indulging it, Odysseus risks life and limb and causes great harm to others.

At other times, Odysseus recognizes that his men can be dangerous or even mutinous. He learns that if he gives them free rein they will prevent him from reaching home. Therefore, single-minded as he is, he must come apart from them. By the end of his travels, Odysseus will have survived many dangerous encounters, but he will have lost all of his crew members and grieved the loss of life. On a symbolic level, he will have shed the negative aspects of his character that these crew members represent, and he will have achieved a greater degree of internal balance.

Odysseus is warned more than once that he will suffer on his journey. Troubles and suffering are part of the human equation. As this book and the story of Odysseus demonstrate, we too can be armed with awareness of the pitfalls and trials we will face on our own journey. We can go within, study our personality and inner being, learn from the patterns we discover, change our ways and overcome the aspects of our character that are keeping us from having and doing what we really desire.

We are all many-faceted beings. We all have "crew members," character traits that we have created and cultivated. These unhelpful traits will not help us reach our goals. They are parts of our being that we would do well to stop cultivating. We all also have positive traits and strengths of character. If we choose to cultivate them, we will increase our internal balance and self-mastery. These strengths are aspects of our higher self and they will help us to achieve our dreams.

MAKING AMENDS

In the opening scene, Zeus proclaims before a gathering of gods on Mount Olympus, "Oh for shame, how the mortals put the blame upon us gods, for they say evils come from us, but it is they, rather, who by their own recklessness win sorrow beyond what is given!" (I:32–34) The concept that what we send out into the world comes back to us is one of Homer's dominant themes in the *Odyssey*. Throughout Odysseus' journey, he reaps the consequences of his actions. In the process, he learns a better way to be in the world.

This applies to us as well. For example, if we

hurt someone's feelings through harsh words or if we lie or cheat to get what we want, we have an internal need, whether we are aware of it or not, to correct these actions in order to make things right. Newton's third law of motion states: "For every action there is an equal and opposite reaction." In other words, whatever we do will eventually come back to us for resolution. There are many idioms and metaphors for this concept: What goes around comes around. Like attracts like. You reap what you sow. Karma. Cause and effect.

But what about a tragic illness, the loss of a loved one, a serious accident or a brutal attack? Is someone's lot always a return of what they have sent out? Not necessarily. While a negative circumstance in our life could be a return of what we have sent out in the past, this is not always the case.

One of the best ways to explain this concept is with the principle of magnetism. Magnets contain iron and they possess the magnetic property of attracting iron. Imagine that you are standing in a room and wearing a magnet when pieces of iron are suddenly thrown into the room. These pieces are of all sizes and shapes, from the finest filings to large chunks. Depending on the size of the magnet you are wearing, you will attract more or less of this debris. If you are not wearing a magnet but happen to be in the way of the debris that comes flying in, it will not cling to you but you might still get hit by the barrage.

To draw an analogy, we could say that every one of us is wearing a magnet that consists of our unique character traits, our strengths and weaknesses, our habits and momentums. In the same way that a magnet attracts iron, the magnet we are wearing attracts both negative and positive experiences. And again, a particular experience might still come to us, as trial or blessing, whether or not we have a magnet for it.

The equations of life are complex. We all have free will, and in the course of living our life we set new consequences in motion with each act, each choice we make. So whether a particular circumstance represents justice or it *just is* because life is testing us, our response to life's challenges is our choice.

Whatever the underlying reasons, some trials can be very hard to accept. Odysseus grieves the loss of each of his companions and the long separation from his homeland. Grieving is appropriate. And as many who have experienced loss and severe challenges have found, we can also choose, as Odysseus does, to accept life's circumstances, adapt, and keep moving forward. In the tempering fires of pain and troubles, we can change and grow.

This is no easy task! But we *can* navigate through the muddy waters of our circumstances as long as we are determined to resolve the internal struggles that beset us. The question is: Are we willing to keep moving through life's trials to return home, to become whole?

FORGIVING THE PAST

Throughout your voyage of self-discovery, be kind to yourself. Forgive yourself for whatever has gone before. Do not get lost in shame and criticism. Forgiveness of ourselves and others is not easy, but forgiveness is essential to building character. Unless we forgive ourselves for past actions, we may condemn or belittle ourselves. If we refuse to forgive another who has wronged us or someone we care about, we tie ourselves to the negative emotions of the situation. Until we resolve the anger, resentment, and hurt, and make peace with the situation, we will not be free.

There may be times when we feel we cannot forgive someone because the act seems too serious. It can be a very hard thing to forgive certain actions taken by people. It can be hard to forgive a child molester who has taken something of the soul of a child that may not be regained. It can be hard to forgive a murderer, a rapist, or one who sets fire to a house or destroys a business. It can be hard to make peace with the loss of a child or a spouse or a loved one, whether through illness or another reason. If we can understand the anatomy of misdeeds, we may find it easier to practice forgiveness in good conscience, with profound sincerity, and without holding anything back. In difficult situations, this means forgiving an individual for acting from the lesser self.

As we explore the trials of Odysseus, we will see his lesser self committing misdeeds and making errors in judgment. Sometimes the choices he makes bring great harm to others. They also bring more hardship to him. But through living with the consequences of his actions, Odysseus learns and grows. He bounces back from mistakes and does not dwell on the past. He moves forward with courage.

If we can see life as a process of maturing, a process of a soul's learning and growing over time, then we may find a way to forgive those whose actions have brought great suffering and grief to us. Like Odysseus, all of us are learning to navigate the waters of life with more self-mastery, more self-control, more grace. No matter what has gone before, we all have the potential to grow and to integrate qualities of our higher self into our thoughts, emotions, words and deeds.

Another reason to forgive is that hatred binds, but love frees. When we can find it in our heart to forgive, we rise above the situation. By forgiving the perpetrator of a terrible deed, we free the energy that has been locked inside the memory of that incident. That energy then becomes available to us for use in more productive ways.

WHEN THE PUPIL IS READY, THE TEACHER APPEARS

On a voyage of self-discovery and inner transformation, it can help to have the support and guidance of someone with a larger perspective, someone who has undertaken a similar odyssey and can guide us along the way. These are the wise ones in our lives who offer encouragement and hold the vision of who we are becoming even when we have temporarily lost that vision for ourselves. Many names are given to these wise souls: mentor, guru, confidant, guide, master and teacher.

Odysseus' teacher is the mythological goddess Athena, daughter of Zeus. Homer portrays Athena as Odysseus' guide and friend. Although Odysseus later complains to her that she was sorely absent during his most difficult trials, she replies that she has been aware of his progress throughout his journey. In fact, has worked behind the scenes to get him back on track.

Athena states, "The gods will not do for man what man must do for himself."[1] In other words, it is up to us to take action. After all, we have spent years developing the various aspects of our personality, our positive and negative traits, and it is up to us to choose to redirect our energy into qualities and characteristics that will serve us better. Again, this is not a punishment. Rather, it is an opportunity to awaken. When we ask to be more courageous in life, we are not magically more courageous. What we find instead are more situations that require us to be courageous. Better stated, we encounter more opportunities to choose to be courageous.

Homeric scholar Howard Clarke writes: "Athena protects Odysseus because he has the skill and cleverness and strength that are also her characteristics.... When a Homeric hero is assisted by a god it is not a sign that he is weak, but rather that he is strong."[2]

We all need the support of those who have stood where we now stand and can offer guidance for our journey. And whether or not we have a flesh-and-blood mentor or guide on our odyssey, we all have an inner teacher, a higher self. This is the voice of conscience that gently prompts us, that guides, warns and comforts us on our odyssey through life. In addition, the voice of wise counsel may come to us in the form of a book, lecture or film, in a conversation with a friend or a chance meeting with a stranger. What we receive from that encounter may provide us with or lead us to the very insight we need to move forward with greater clarity and belief in ourselves.

"CLOCKING" THE JOURNEY

As we follow Odysseus in his journey, we can imagine that we are Odysseus, facing off with mythical beasts and passing through treacherous straits. Or we can imagine that we are at his side, a supportive companion witnessing firsthand the struggles he faces. Or perhaps we would prefer, from the safety of an armchair, to observe him through a looking glass in order to learn what patterns we can discover beneath his fantastic adventures. We can then study these underlying patterns to decipher how each one relates to us and to the tests of character we face.

Homer's insight into human nature is as relevant today as it was nearly three thousand years ago. Odysseus undergoes archetypal trials, each focusing on one aspect of his character. The trials he faces are universal tests. Within them we will find echoes of our own patterns, as if Homer had written the story just for us.

Our symbolic journey with Odysseus will be taken one key episode at a time, starting when he leaves Ithaca and concluding when he returns to his family, home and kingdom. We will review his adventures as a linear, step-by-step journey, each trial being neatly bound within the confines of a test of one archetypal quality or character trait. However, it will soon become clear that the threads of each trial are intertwined into a single tapestry.

Thus, rather than progressing in linear fashion, the journey is more circular, like a clock. As we follow Odysseus around the clock, moving from one trial to the next, we will notice that his strengths in one area can help him overcome weaknesses in other areas. We will also see that even though he fails some of his early tests, in later episodes he is given another opportunity to pass that test and his actions demonstrate that he has learned the lesson. We will see this demonstrated throughout Odysseus' voyage as he gains increasing self-mastery, and we can also recognize it in our own voyage of self-discovery.

We will study twelve trials contained within twelve episodes. Thus, we can think of these trials as being placed on a clock with the first trial on the twelve o'clock line and the final trial on the eleven o'clock line.

GETTING THE MOST FROM THE *ODYSSEY*

With each of Odysseus' trials, you will discover if and how the underlying patterns in Odysseus' trials relate to you personally. As you review his trials, you may identify traits you want to work on and convert into strengths. You will also discover areas where you already shine, positive aspects and qualities you already embody.

Each chapter includes a chart of strengths and weaknesses for the archetypal quality of that trial. Take time to consider which of these aspects best fit you. If you want another perspective, ask a trusted friend to gently share how they see you in relation to these qualities. The more honest you are with yourself, the better you will be able to anticipate the pitfalls and opportunities you will encounter on your journey.

The traits you identify are your map of your inner self as of that day, a snapshot in time. At a later date the weaknesses that you identify with today may change and become fewer, because by putting your attention on them and striving, you will have transformed more of them into positive expressions.

Tests of character pop up in everyday living. They may appear, for example, as a temptation to procrastinate, to lie, to cheat, to feel irritated, or to get even. You will also notice positive patterns that repeat and grow richer and fuller, strengths such as the tendency to offer kind words or to help others, to be an effective leader, to see projects through to completion, to be a peacemaker, to bring beauty and order to your surroundings.

Also included in the discussion of each trial are Winning Strategies for anchoring and acting on your insights. Some of these you may have heard about and may already be using. Others may be new to you. They are all practical keys for making positive change.

Each chapter offers questions for self-reflection. These are grouped under two headings: "Who Am I?" and "Where Am I Going?"

As you explore your inner world, you will also discover qualities and traits not addressed in these pages. There are, of course, many important strengths and weaknesses besides the ones that are discussed in this book. As other qualities come to mind, make note of them. Track your progress in expressing them in positive ways. Above all, take comfort in knowing that your higher self is already within you. You have within you the stuff it takes to be the hero or heroine of your own story. Take heart. Hold fast, seek true friendship, and keep the vision.

LOVE WILL BRING YOU HOME

As you go through these episodes of the Odyssey, you will discover your unique blend of qualities. Reflect on the overall patterns. Some of us, for example, may be good at wielding power but fall short in tempering it with love and wisdom. We may display wisdom but be timid or stingy about sharing it with others. Or perhaps we are loving and compassionate but lacking in discipline or discernment.

Odysseus struggles until he masters the aspects of his lesser self that are keeping him from reaching home. Once he achieves a good balance by transforming weak points in his character into strengths, his final trial goes like clockwork.

We all have weak points that hinder us from making progress in our soul's odyssey. Once we identify these characteristics, we can begin to transform them into their positive counterparts. We all also have strong points that we can use to bring ourselves into greater balance. Our strengths are our foundation. They will help to take us successfully through the trials we encounter on our voyage of self-discovery.

Odysseus does not tackle all his flaws at once and neither do we need to. Like him, we can take on one test of character at a time. Some of us will decide to begin with the trait that holds us back the most. Others of us might choose to work first on those we can most readily commit to overcoming.

Tracking your progress by acknowledging and celebrating your victories, both big and small, will encourage you to keep going. It will help you to build a momentum of overcoming and victory. Writing down your victories as well as the insights that come to you will allow you to refer back to your notes when your journey gets tough.

In a sense, these twelve trials are all about the victory of love. Love is Odysseus' key to meeting every one of his challenges. His love for his family and homeland, for his companions, for himself and for the person he is becoming are what keep him striving to reach home and, symbolically, to become his higher self.

And so it is for us: Our love for ourselves, our humanity, our family and friends, and for who we are becoming will help us to pass our tests of character. Let us meet our challenges with love and compassion for ourselves and others. Doing so will help us to let go of any attachment to past mistakes and allow us to keep moving forward. Ultimately, it is love that will bring us home to our higher self and help us reach our highest goals.

ONLY THE ENERGY OF THE HEART
MAKES A MAN INVULNERABLE AND CARRIES
HIM OVER OBSTACLES.

HELENA ROERICH

Twelve o'Clock Line

THRUST OF POWER

FOLLOWING
THE ROUTE OF
ODYSSEUS

Twelve o'Clock Line

THRUST OF POWER

*I myself, I know no sweeter sight on earth
than a man's own native country.*
ODYSSEUS

Our journey with Odysseus begins with the events
that lead him to the mythical adventures described in the
Odyssey.

Odysseus is the king of Ithaca, an island off the
west coast of Greece. He is married to Penelope, who has
just borne him a son. Just when everything seems to be
going well for him, a catastrophe hits the Greek world.
Helen, the beautiful wife of the Spartan king Menelaus, is
abducted, perhaps with her consent, by Paris, a prince of
Troy.

Kings and princes of the various Greek states,
having made an earlier pact to stand by Helen's husband,
prepare to set sail for Troy to force her return. A vast
Greek fleet gathers, but Odysseus is missing. An oracle
has told Odysseus that if he goes to Troy he will not

return for twenty years and will arrive home alone and destitute. No wonder he is resistant to leave.

Odysseus' participation in the war is crucial to the Greeks and they are convinced that they cannot win the war without him. For Odysseus is renowned as a master strategist and as the most clever and ingenious of the Greek kings and warriors. The Greeks value Odysseus' participation so greatly that they delay the campaign to Troy while Menelaus and others sail to Ithaca to urge Odysseus to join them. Finally, he agrees to fight. He gathers twelve ships of Ithacans under his command and leaves home thoroughly committed to a Greek victory.

The oracle warns Odysseus that he will not return for twenty years if he leaves for Troy.

Odysseus, the most clever and ingenious of the Greek kings and warriors.

In the tenth year of the long and grueling war, Achilles, the greatest warrior among the Greeks, is slain. Discouraged, the Greeks prepare to return home. The goddess Athena intervenes, directing Odysseus to rally the men. He inspires the Greek armies to continue fighting but the war remains at a stalemate.

Inspired once again by Athena, Odysseus conceives an ingenious ruse to get Greek warriors inside the walls of Troy. His cunning and bravery prove invaluable. He directs the Greeks to build a huge wooden horse with a trap door. He and several warriors hide in its hollow belly. The Greek ships sail far enough out of sight to allow the main contingent of the army to go into hiding, ready at a moment's notice to storm the citadel of Troy.

To all appearances, the Greeks have given up and sailed for home, abandoning the massive wooden horse

The Trojans drag the wheeled horse, with Odysseus and his warriors within its hollow belly, inside their gates.

on the shore. The Trojans take the bait. They drag the wheeled horse inside their gates, then celebrate until they fall into an exhausted sleep. When all is still in Troy, the hidden warriors sneak out of the horse, open the city gates and let in the main Greek army. They reclaim Helen but they do not stop there. The Greeks burn and sack Troy and butcher the men. They load their ships with the spoils of Troy.

Even for those rough times, the Greeks go too far. The gods who have helped the Greeks all along are offended by the wanton violence, wild looting and slaughter. As the victorious Greeks depart Troy to return home, they are afflicted with hardships by Zeus, chief deity and god of the sky and weather. Some die en route. Others encounter varying degrees of difficulty either before arriving home or after. But no one faces more challenges than Odysseus and his crew.

Odysseus sets out for home with twelve ships filled with booty from the sack of Troy. He longs to be reunited with his faithful wife, Penelope, whom he loves dearly, and his son, who was just an infant when Odysseus left for the war. But for all of his victories and cleverness in battle, Odysseus is not destined to see Ithaca again just yet. He has some important lessons to learn, and he must also make amends for his excesses and abuses of power. The gods will not allow him to reach home until he learns those lessons.

Let us now explore the inner meaning of the trials of Odysseus and learn from them how we can prepare for and pass our own tests on our journey to wholeness.

THE PRICE OF VICTORY

Twelve o'clock, where we begin our inner journey with Odysseus, signifies the start of a new day, the beginning of a new cycle, the thrust of a new venture. All new ventures call for sustained willpower and drive. Odysseus has these traits and more.

To accept the heroic call to fight at Troy, Odysseus has to summon tremendous inner strength, courage and determination. Imagine what it must take for him to leave home in spite of the oracle's warning that he will not return for twenty years.

He hesitates. He has a comfortable lifestyle. He is the ruler of a kingdom, a strong, well-respected leader.

His wife and his people love him. But go he must and he accepts the challenge. Once he does, he is fully committed. His ambition and drive keep him one-pointed on his goal: winning the war against Troy. He swiftly summons his countrymen, mans and arms twelve ships, and sets sail.

After the fall of Troy, Odysseus' determined thrust to return home to his beloved wife and son and to his duties as king becomes an entirely new and unexpected venture. While this seems at the outset to be a relatively simple undertaking, it will take all of his resources to achieve this goal.

Symbolically, Odysseus is on an inner journey to wholeness. Reclaiming his rightful place in his home and kingdom represents his completion of his sojourn. He completes the circle of his journey, returning to his starting point but with a higher level of wholeness. It signifies the transformation of his lesser self, the negative or unhelpful aspects of his character, into their positive counterparts, aspects of his higher self. As we will see, when Odysseus does complete his journey, he will have integrated many aspects of his higher self.

The challenge for Odysseus is not only to leave a comfortable or familiar lifestyle to serve a cause. It is the challenge to engage in an internal adventure. Odysseus' going off to war and his return voyage home symbolize the courage, discipline and determination it takes to embark upon a spiritual journey, to fight the internal battles that will lead to inner balance and wholeness.

Like Odysseus, we may at times feel overcome by inertia because we fear what a new venture will bring. After considering our options we too may hesitate. Will we decide to take up the journey determined to win all the way? Will we have the willpower and drive to bring all our abilities to bear to secure our victory, to come full circle and make it all the way home, come what may? That is the key.

To embark on a voyage of self-discovery takes consciously choosing to look inward, to go within and uproot concepts, thoughts and desires that are no longer useful to us. When we clear out negative emotions and memories from the past, when we discard erroneous beliefs that no longer serve us, we create a clean slate. We make room for the ideas, concepts, knowledge and desires that relate to what we truly desire and are determined to manifest as our most important gift to society, that which we will leave as our legacy.

To have our victory and achieve our major goals in life we may need to travel, take a course, earn a degree or master a skill or trade in order to make them a reality. Like the journey of Odysseus, our voyage of self-discovery will be marked by challenges. Expect them. Get ready for them.

POWER—THE WIND IN OUR SAILS

The facets of Odysseus' character that we have discussed thus far are, in a sense, all aspects of power. Power is the wind in our sails that allows us to embark on a new venture and to see it through to completion.

In this first trial, the challenge for Odysseus and for each of us is to learn the right use of power. This means tempering power with love and wisdom to achieve our goals without causing harm to anyone. Do we wield power wisely and with compassion? Are we sensitive to others? Or do we use power and people ruthlessly, with blind ambition, crushing whatever stands in the way of our getting what we want?

How does Odysseus use power? He uses the Trojan War as an opportunity to establish his status and reputation. He is practical and a good leader. He uses power to come up with effective strategies that help to win the war. But in this trial he does not pass all his tests. At the end of the war, sorely lacking in love and discriminating wisdom, Odysseus and the Greeks abuse their power by sacking Troy and butchering the men. Their goal was to liberate Helen and perhaps to punish the Trojans, but not to destroy Troy. The consequences of their tremendous abuse of power will unfold throughout the outer drama.

The warriors' abuse of power is a strong "masculine" expression. Qualities that are traditionally considered to be masculine are action- and goal-oriented, practical and analytical. In both men and women, the "masculine" side is the side that protects, disciplines, sets standards and enforces limits. Odysseus has a well-developed masculine side, as do his crew members. On a symbolic level they represent aspects of Odysseus' personality.

But Odysseus' strong masculine personality is not in balance with what, traditionally, are the "feminine" qualities, such as compassion, intuition and emotional sensitivity. The "feminine" side of both man and woman nurtures, teaches, supports, comforts and heals. Many of the later tests Odysseus faces involve women. Each of these women also symbolizes a part of his personality that he must recognize and deal with.

To be whole, Odysseus must integrate and balance

the masculine and feminine aspects. When we act from a place of wholeness, our actions uplift us and others. In fact, when we criticize or condemn others, it is often because we feel powerless. The act of putting down someone else may temporarily make us feel elevated and powerful. But putting down anyone is really an admission that we ourselves are not whole.

Self-condemnation is another aspect of this pattern. On our voyage of self-discovery, if we become aware that we frequently display a certain negative trait or if we make the same mistake again and again, we may feel discouraged. At times like these it can be helpful to remind ourselves that the journey to integrate aspects of our higher self is a process of fine-tuning. Self-examination for the purpose of inner growth is healthy; condemning ourselves for our shortcomings or perceived failures is not.

The first step to breaking the pattern of condemning ourselves and others is to become conscious of what we are doing. The next step is to look within to discover the reasons why we are engaging in this behavior and to understand what benefit we think we are gaining from doing it.

As we resolve the underlying issues, we will no longer be so sensitive to our own mistakes and shortcomings or to the perceived flaws of others. After all, the faults we see in others are often a magnified reflection of our own unresolved issues. When we feel loved, we feel no need to condemn others. As we heal our inner being, we extend love to others. Over time they, too, will feel loved, and their need to condemn others will also lessen. Love really is the fulfilling of the law of life.

HOW PASSION RELATES TO POWER

Odysseus makes bold decisions and pursues them with passion. He harnesses and directs his lesser desires in pursuit of his foremost goal. His desire to succeed is strong and it gives him staying power in difficult trials.

Those who get the most out of life tend to be those who pursue their goals with passion. There is nothing lukewarm about their journey. Nothing distracts them from their goals, at least not for long. Through thick or thin, they retain their passion and drive. When Odysseus' indulgence in a lesser desire takes him temporarily off course, his intense passion to reach Ithaca drives him, sooner or later, to self-correct.

This is the essence of power that we want in our lives. The essence of a thing is its heart. To embody the essence of power, the kind of power that will help us to achieve our most cherished goals, we have to know what power looks and feels like in its most positive expression. We also have to want it with a passion.

Many people find it difficult to realistically define a mission and vision statement for themselves. They might say they want to have a mansion, plenty of money, go here, do this, have that. But they have a harder time defining what it is that they want more than anything, what it is that will drive their lives with passion so that they can create and fulfill their unique legacy, their gift to life.

Travel, experiences and material possessions may come to us or not in the course of fulfilling our destiny, but the acquisition of things does not define a mission. To discover our mission, our destiny in life, we must go to the core of our being, to the wellspring of life from whence issues the energy, consciousness, determination and excitement to transcend our lesser self, achieve our goals, and become one with our higher self.

☉ ANCHORING YOUR INSIGHTS ☉

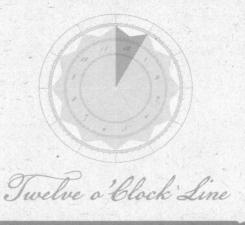

Twelve o'Clock Line

TESTS OF POWER

STRENGTHS	WEAKNESSES
healthy ambition, strong desire to succeed	blind ambition, ruthlessness, suspicion
practical, organized, efficient, cautious	sense of limitation or restriction; overly hesitant
hardworking, patient in pursuit of goals	pessimistic, depressed
leadership capacity	criticizes or condemns when feeling powerless
self-disciplined, responsible, has a sense of duty	intolerant, stubborn, harsh
power tempered with love and wisdom	exploitation or abuse of power; arbitrary or despotic

WHO AM I?
TWELVE O'CLOCK LINE: POWER

Take a moment to think about power in your life. Reflect on the chart of strengths and weaknesses and use it to evaluate your expressions of power. Later in this chapter, you will have an opportunity to map your strategy for turning weaknesses into strengths.

What are my greatest strengths in relation to power?

_____

_____

_____

What are my greatest weaknesses in relation to power?

_____

_____

_____

Thus far in my life, how have I handled challenges involving aspects of power? Would I handle any of those situations differently now? How?

_____

_____

_____

What can I learn about myself and power from Odysseus' experience? Am I hesitating to embark upon any important part of my personal odyssey?

_____

_____

_____

WINNING STRATEGIES
TWELVE O'CLOCK LINE: POWER

CLAIM YOUR POWER. There will be times when you will need a tremendous amount of fortitude to overcome whatever challenge you are dealing with. You may not feel that you have the will power to affirm something and stay with it. You may think someone with more power has to do it for you. But we are all empowered people.

You were born empowered and you can claim your power any time you decide.

LET YOUR HIGHER SELF LEAD. Putting energy into negative habits or character traits is a misuse of power. We all have within us the power to kick whatever habit we are determined to overcome. To begin, determine that you *will* overcome it and give yourself a timeline. If you slip, affirm your resolve and start over. If you slip again, reaffirm your resolve and keep moving forward. Staying on track gets easier over time. Believe it.

Maintaining your resolve takes regular exercising in order to keep it strong. It is just like exercising a muscle that you have not used in a while. At first the muscle is weak. But over time, as you continue to exercise it, that muscle grows stronger and stronger.

When you resolve to embody the higher aspects of self, your higher self will take you where you need to be.

LOVE YOUR HIGHER SELF MORE THAN ANYTHING ELSE. When we love, we are sensitive to others. Consider how children tease one another. Whether it is intended or not, sometimes the teasing can really hurt. Most of us do not think of ourselves as abusive, but it is possible to abuse power in many ways, some of them subtle. One example is "getting even" with somebody. When our heart is filled with love, we no longer feel a need to get even or to abuse others.

When you love the higher aspects of your being, your higher self, more than anything else, you get it all back. That is why love is the ultimate empowerment.

TURN DRIVE INTO STAYING POWER. Studying the lives of great men and women shows us how they expressed the positive attributes of power. Typically, we find the great ones to be down to earth and practical. Many of them expressed their love in a practical way through their works.

When you understand the daunting challenges you must pass through to achieve your goals, you too may hesitate, as Odysseus did. You may feel pessimistic or limited. If you succumb to these feelings, you may procrastinate or begin your project or endeavor halfheartedly.

If you recognize this tendency in yourself, the antidote is to turn yourself around and start over. If your goals are realistic and achievable and you have laid out a clear, practical plan for accomplishing them, then you know you can keep going. You can turn yourself around three or four times if you have to.

The key is to not quit striving until you achieve your goal.

FORGIVE YOURSELF AND OTHERS. Many of us find it difficult to forgive. Nonforgiveness, whether of ourselves or another, keeps us stuck in condemnation. Sometimes self-condemnation poses as self-discipline and it can overflow, causing us to condemn others. It is a distortion of the golden rule wherein we say, "I do it to myself, so I'll do it to everyone."

If you don't realize that you are condemning yourself, you aren't likely to notice that you are doing it to others. The key to overcoming this harmful trait is forgiveness. Forgiveness contains the quality of mercy—mercy for oneself and mercy for others.

As you forgive yourself and others, you start a new life.

WHERE AM I GOING?
TWELVE O'CLOCK LINE: POWER

As you reflect on the following questions, you may find it helpful to review the various aspects of power in the chart on p. 34 and "The Stuff Heroes Are Made Of" on pp. 4–5, as well as the Winning Strategies. Using the questions below, map out a strategy to apply the insights you've gained.

Have I made the conscious choice to embark on a victorious odyssey to becoming whole and balanced, one with my higher self?

_____

_____

In the tests of power of my current life circumstances, how can I use my strengths constructively?

_____

_____

_____

How can I turn any weakness I may have into an expression of power that I can claim as a new strength?

_____

_____

_____

What is it that will drive my life with passion to create and fulfill my unique legacy? How can I focus power to succeed?

_____

_____

_____

To reach the port...
we must sail sometimes with the wind
and sometimes against it—
but we must sail, and not drift,
nor lie at anchor.

Oliver Wendell Holmes

BULGARIA

STAR...

Kazan

Komotini

Istanbul

Maronia

Canakkale

Troy

GREECE

END

TUR

Athens

Mycenae

Pylos

Sparta

Crete

One o'Clock Line

A CHANCE TO CHAMPION LOVE

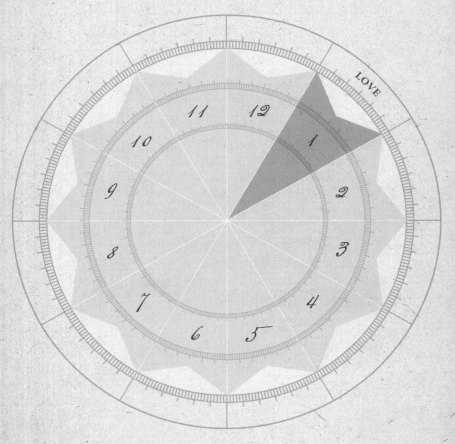

One o'Clock Line

LOVE

11 12 1
10   2
9   3
8   4
7 6 5

A CHANCE TO CHAMPION LOVE

The wind took me and drove me ashore
at Ismaros by the Kikonians.
I sacked their city and killed their people.
ODYSSEUS

After the fall of Troy, Odysseus sets sail for home with twelve ships of Ithacans. They are intoxicated by the victory in Troy and feelings of newfound freedom. The prevailing winds drive them to Ismaros, the stronghold of the Kikonians. Odysseus and his crew plunder the city of Ismaros, indulging their lowest desires. Odysseus tells the story: "I sacked their city and killed their people, and out of their city taking their wives and many possessions we shared them out, so that none might go cheated of his proper portion." (IX:40–43)

Although piracy was common in those times, Odysseus realizes they have gone too far. After the raid he tells his men, "Back, and quickly! Out to sea again!"

(IX:43–44) But his crew members are mutinous fools. Odysseus recalls:

> There was too much wine to swill, too many sheep to slaughter down along the beach, and shambling long-horn cattle. And all the while the Kikonians sought out other Kikonians, called for help from their neighbors living inland: a larger force, and stronger soldiers too, skilled hands at fighting men from chariots, skilled, when a crisis broke, to fight on foot. Out of the morning mist they came against us—packed as the leaves and spears that flower forth in spring—and Zeus presented us with disaster, me and my comrades doomed to suffer blow on mortal blow. (IX:45–53)

Odysseus loses six companions out of each ship, seventy-two in all. He and the remaining Ithacans flee from the destruction, "glad to have escaped death, but grieving still at heart for the loss of our dear companions." (IX:62–63)

LOVE UPHOLDS FREEDOM

Immediately upon setting sail for home, Odysseus and his companions begin reaping the consequences of their brutal actions in Troy even as they continue to add to their troubles. The prevailing winds, rather than taking them toward Ithaca, blow them off course.

In this trial, Odysseus is tested with regard to the archetypal quality of love. Within the many facets of love is a related quality, freedom, for if we genuinely love others, we cherish and uphold their freedom as well as our

Odysseus retells battling the Kikonians: "Out of the morning mist they came against us...and Zeus presented us with disaster, me and my comrades doomed to suffer blow on mortal blow."

own. In the city of Ismaros, as in the last days in Troy, Odysseus and his crew ruthlessly pursue their own wanton desires. In plundering, taking lives and enslaving others, they abuse their freedom by violating the liberty of others. In effect, they play out a classic but potentially inappropriate impulse: "I want to do my own thing my own way and nothing is going to stop me."

The retribution is swift and staggering—the loss of half of Odysseus' companions, a huge setback for the voyage home. "Zeus presented us with disaster," Odysseus says. We can view the loss as a return of the negative energy the Ithacans have sent out in their treatment of the Trojans and Kikonians. "What goes around comes around."

In this episode we see that the expression of freedom without compassion, tolerance and sensitivity to the needs, feelings and rights of others is destructive, not only to those around us but also, in the final analysis, to ourselves. If we are not our brother's keeper, if we do not show care for our neighbor, we will in reality gain nothing ourselves. In fact, we will set ourselves back, as Odysseus does, because acting with an unloving, destructive attitude sets in motion negative circumstances that will sooner or later come back to us. It is impossible to truly succeed if we do not also include success for our fellowman in our plans.

Odysseus and his crew continue to demonstrate their strong masculine side in their prowess as warriors. At the same time, they expose their weakness on the feminine side through their ruthless treatment of the Kikonians. The energy behind riding roughshod over others is a heart that is not softened, a lack of balance in the inner being. Wholeness contains a balance between masculine and feminine qualities. Again, these are not yet in balance in Odysseus. Before he again sets foot in his homeland, he must achieve a greater degree of inner balance. He is still a long way from the "home" of oneness with his higher self.

If we look at Odysseus' crew members and those he encounters as representing various aspects of his negative character traits and weaknesses, then the loss of his companions can be taken symbolically to mean that he must transform his negative traits into a higher expression. Significantly, when Odysseus does reach home after his long round-trip journey, he will arrive alone, indicating that he is no longer split, but "all one." Indeed, by then he will have integrated many positive character traits.

THE VALUE OF TEAMWORK

Another test Odysseus receives in this episode has to do with cooperation, teamwork and forming alliances. Odysseus does just the opposite with the Kikonians. When Odysseus arrives at Ismaros, he acts from lower desires. He has been at war for ten years and has not yet learned a new way of being. He leads his companions, his team, in a successful attack on the Kikonians. He heeds the inner voice that warns him of imminent danger by giving the command to get back to the ships and depart quickly. But then he is conflicted. His crew members insist on remaining on the island and reveling, and he gives in.

Here, Odysseus can be seen as giving in to the desires of his lesser self instead of obeying the lead of his higher self. In consequence, he loses half of his men. Our crafty warrior is learning the hard way that reliance on brute force and on his own ego is not enough to carry him home. Although he does not pass this test, he is receiving a valuable lesson in teamwork.

A harmonious team that works toward a common goal can get a job done faster by pooling the resources and abilities of all members under a strong leader. By assigning team members to contribute where they have abilities, everyone benefits. This is because everyone on a team has something of value to contribute.

To sum it up, in this trial Odysseus is tested on his handling of the qualities of love and its corollary, freedom. In leading the attack on the Kikonians, he and his men show themselves to be heartless, insensitive and willing to violate others to get what they want. Odysseus then gives his men too much freedom by ignoring his own inner leader, his intuition, in a critical moment. As a result, he fails to lead them all to safety. In effect, by giving them what they wanted without discerning and giving them what they needed, he lets them down. He then has to deal with the consequences of his behavior.

The return attack on his army and the loss of many men provides him with an opportunity to integrate the lessons of this trial. By realizing that what he imposes upon others can interfere with his important plans and higher desires, he will begin to appreciate the value of remaining aware and being considerate of what others need. He is also learning that in order to keep his companions safe he must let his inner voice be the strong leader.

BECOMING LOVE

Perfect love is not easy to attain, yet in order to truly enjoy an ideal love, we must become love. Love can be tender and gentle. It can be as powerful as the creation of an entire cosmos. Love must be tempered in our hearts, in our daily doings and expressions, in our giving to life.

Since love is tender and yet a two-edged sword, love requires that we listen to our hearts. When we do not listen within, when we do not commune with our inner heart and soul, we become vulnerable to falling into a trap of hatred of self or of others. This includes not only full-blown hatred but also mild dislike and hardness of heart. Within the seed lies the whole plant; thus mild dislike, if not checked, can grow like a poisonous weed into hatred and brutality.

In his trial, Odysseus ignores his inner prompting to escape quickly from Ismaros, heeding instead his men's desire to feast and drink. When reveling turns to disaster, he blames his crew: "There I was for the light foot and escaping, and urged it, but they were greatly foolish and would not listen." (IX:43, 44) In a sense, he projects onto his men his dislike of his decision to indulge his lesser self.

Dislike is subtle, because it seems innocuous. For example, we might tell ourselves, "I don't care for that individual, but so what—it's not important." But it *is* important. If we have even mild dislike for anyone, we can be certain that we dislike some aspect of ourselves. We tend to project our dislike for our own unacknowledged or unresolved character traits onto others who exhibit those same traits. The antidote, the path to love, is through finding inner resolution.

We hear people talk about speaking from the heart and acting from the heart. Yet real love is not sentimental or passive. It is strong. It is soft. And it is eminently practical. The strong points of love are often spoken of as "tough love." Those who raise children understand the process of bringing children to higher and higher levels of personal responsibility over time. This is the love that moves an adult to keep a child and an entire family in balance.

If Odysseus had shown tough love in this episode by following his inner prompting and commanding his men to escape while there was yet time, he could have led them to safety. This would have shown true compassion. By indulging them sympathetically instead of compassionately holding the line, he passively allowed them to fail. As a result, half of his men met their doom.

The way to develop any quality is to cultivate the various positive aspects and expressions of it until we so fully embody them that we have displaced the negatives. Every one of the archetypal qualities in the trials of Odysseus is one that will serve us well as we approach and pass through the gate of higher consciousness. For example, we can only get through the gate of love by mastering love, by becoming love. We can only transmute the antithesis of love with love.

As mentioned earlier, the tests of character that we face on our journey to wholeness are part of a process of fine-tuning. Over time the tests we face become more subtle. For example, someone who has consistently behaved in a loving manner may suddenly find welling up from within an intense emotion or feeling that they had never been aware of until then. They may encounter someone who represents for them an obstacle they have with regard to some aspect of love, something they must tackle and overcome. In response, they may feel disdain or dislike for the other person instead of acknowledging the situation as a reflection of their own unresolved issue.

This is the kind of subtle opportunity that can present itself to us. If we are aware in that moment, we are more likely to recognize the situation and our reaction to it as something we must deal with in order to make progress on our odyssey. Happy are we who can see situations like this as opportunities to choose love and to strive to become love.

⚜ ANCHORING YOUR INSIGHTS ☯

One o'Clock Line

TESTS OF LOVE

STRENGTHS	WEAKNESSES
champions freedom for self and others; independent	violates freedom of others; unpredictable, rebellious
broadminded, egalitarian; gives liberating information	tactless, argumentative, opinionated
loving, friendly; team player; forms networks	hardhearted, detached, coldly intellectual
humanitarian, idealistic	impersonal, self-centered
original, intuitive, open to new ideas	overly eccentric; enjoys shocking people
determined, firm, analytical	stubborn, unwilling to change

WHO AM I?
ONE O'CLOCK LINE: LOVE

Take a moment to think about love in your life. Reflect on the chart of strengths and weaknesses and use it to evaluate your expressions of love. Later in this chapter, you will have an opportunity to map your strategy for turning weaknesses into strengths.

What are my greatest strengths in relation to love?

_____

_____

_____

What are my greatest weaknesses in relation to love, especially concerning sensitivity to the personal needs of others?

_____

_____

_____

Thus far in my life, how have I handled challenges involving aspects of love? Would I handle any of those situations differently now? How?

_____

_____

_____

What can I learn about myself and love from Odysseus' experience?

_____

_____

_____

WINNING STRATEGIES
ONE O'CLOCK LINE: LOVE

EXPRESS YOURSELF IN WAYS YOU WILL NOT REGRET. When you are tempted to engage in the antithesis of love, whether through anger, pride, hatred or another expression, excuse yourself from the scene, take a deep breath, and ask yourself: "If I do this, how will I feel tomorrow morning?"

Love your soul enough to express yourself and your desires in a way that you will not regret.

CONSIDER HOW YOUR ACTIONS WILL AFFECT OTHERS. Before giving free rein to the whim to do things your own way, ask yourself: "How will my actions affect others?" Also ask yourself: "Am I breaking through an internal barrier that is hindering my personal growth or am I just breaking the rules of accepted conduct in order to do things my way?"

Love is sensitive. Consider the impact your actions will have on others.

BE OPEN TO LEARNING FROM EVERYONE AND EVERYTHING. In *The Devil's Dictionary*, Ambrose Bierce sums up the human tendency to stubbornly shut out opposing points of view. He defines the word *ignoramus* this way: "A person unacquainted with certain kinds of knowledge familiar to yourself, and having certain other kinds that you know nothing about."[3]

Avoid the tendency to think that you know all there is to know about something.

GIVE LOVE IN A PERSONAL WAY. Think of the joy a parent derives from receiving a bouquet of flowers that a five-year-old picked by himself. Get in touch with your emotions and learn to give generously on a personal level, even to someone you don't know that well. Doing this makes giving fun. It expands the heart and balances strong masculine energy with the intuitive feminine energy, enhancing your sensitivity to others.

Your love will be felt most when it touches others in a personal way.

GIVE LOVE IN PRACTICAL WAYS. We can all get so caught up in ourselves that we do not notice that the people right in front of us have needs, both great and small, that only we can fill. Our talents and knowledge and the skills we have garnered can help them, so let us be willing to share with others.

At the same time, we cannot give so much at once that we inundate those we are trying to help. The key is to discern what the other person needs right now and to meet that need. This is not about giving everything that we want to communicate or give. Think of it as serving a meal to guests, one course at a time, never forcing more food on them than they want or are ready for.

Love is practical. Develop a heart of compassion by giving to others in practical ways.

WHERE AM I GOING?

ONE O'CLOCK LINE: LOVE

As you reflect on the following questions, you may find it helpful to review the various aspects of love in the chart on p. 53 and "The Stuff Heroes Are Made Of" on pp. 4–5, as well as the Winning Strategies. Using the questions below, map out a strategy to apply the insights you've gained.

In the tests of love presented by my current life circumstances, how can I use my strengths constructively?

_____

_____

_____

How can I turn any weakness I may have into an expression of love that I can claim as a new strength?

_____

_____

_____

Is there an area of my life where I need to express "tough love"? How can I do that, while keeping my masculine and feminine energies balanced?

_____

_____

_____

What are some ways that I could "stretch my wings" to support the freedom of others, even in areas where I may be attached to my own desires?

_____

_____

_____

MASTERING OTHERS IS STRENGTH.
MASTERING YOURSELF IS TRUE POWER.

TAO TE CHING

BULGARIA

START

Komotini

Kecan

Istanbul

Maronia

Canakkale

Troy

GREECE

TUR

END

Athens

Mycenae

Pylos

Sparta

CRETE

FOLLOWING

Two o'Clock Line

MASTERING THE DREAM WORLD

Two o'Clock Line

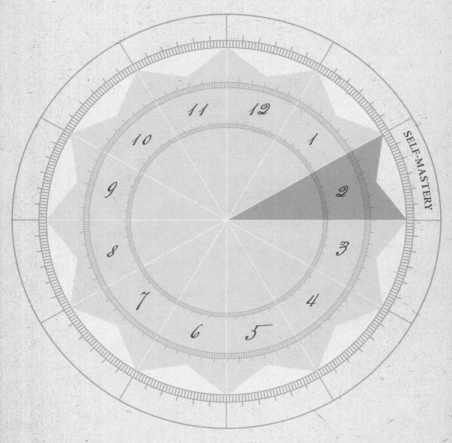

LOTUS EATERS

MASTERING THE DREAM WORLD

*They wanted to stay there with the lotus-eating people
...and forget the way home.*
ODYSSEUS

After fleeing Ismaros, Odysseus and his remaining men sail on until Zeus whips up a storm that rips their sails into pieces. They quickly take down the masts, stow the torn sails, and row to the mainland. "We saw death in that fury," says Odysseus. "Two long days and nights we lay offshore worn out and sick at heart, tasting our grief." (IX:73, 74–75)

On the third day, they hoist their sails and set out for home. They are approaching familiar land when hostile winds and currents take them off course. For nine days the ships are carried on the teeming sea, driven by dangerously high winds.

On the tenth day, they stop at the land of the Lotus Eaters, a people who live on a flowering food.

Odysseus sends three men to find out who the inhabitants of the land are. The people are friendly and offer them the honey-sweet lotus to eat.

Odysseus recalls: "Any of them who ate the honey-sweet fruit of lotus was unwilling to take any message back, or to go away, but they wanted to stay there with the lotus-eating people, feeding on lotus, and forget the way home. I myself took these men back weeping, by force, to where the ships were." (IX:94–98) Odysseus ties them down securely and warns the others not to taste of the lotus for fear of forgetting their home. In haste, Odysseus and his crew depart the idyllic but dangerous land.

OVERCOMING THE DESIRE TO ESCAPE

The archetypal quality of this trial is self-mastery. Tests in this area are often related to a mastery of fear and self-doubt. If we think of Odysseus' crew as representing elements of himself and his adventure as an internal drama, this scene symbolizes Odysseus' fear to move forward with his journey. Small wonder! Odysseus has already had a taste of the challenges of the voyage home and realizes that it is not going to be as easy as he had thought.

One part of Odysseus would rather "bliss out" than continue on a journey that seems doomed to heartbreak and failure. This is his lesser self, represented by the scouting party that eats the lotus, slips into a blissful forgetfulness, and wants to remain in the dream world. But another part of him, his higher self, recognizes the danger. Odysseus must choose which voice to heed. He conquers the temptation and determines to stay on his homeward course.

"They wanted to stay there with the lotus-eating people, feeding on lotus," Odysseus recalls. "I myself took these men back weeping, by force, to where the ships were."

His firm decision is evidenced in his dragging the lotus-eating scouts back to their ship and lashing them securely under their rowing benches. It is also seen in his clear command to the rest: "All hands aboard; come, clear the beach and no one taste the Lotus, or you lose your hope of home." (IX:101–102) This time the men obey without hesitation.

The desire to escape from stressful or difficult circumstances can be a strong temptation. Mastering the desire to escape from reality is a test every one of us will encounter at some point. Will we give up when the going gets tough? Will we settle for living in a dream world? Or, like Odysseus, will we conquer the temptation? Accepting and engaging the reality of life's challenges presents us with opportunities to achieve greater self-mastery.

Often a fear of pain or failure is at the root of escapism. Sometimes that fear stems from a lack of self-confidence. Whatever its source, it can cause us to avoid necessary challenges and to succumb to a dreamlike indolence.

INNER POWER TO MOVE FORWARD

Because fear offers us an excuse not to do something, an excuse to avoid challenges on our odyssey, it can block our victorious journey through life. Fear has many faces, many disguises. Yet, whatever temptation may assail us offering a way to avoid our fears—whether through an addiction or by giving in to a weakness in character or any other means—we have the inner power to choose to keep propelling ourselves forward, as Odysseus does. We *can* walk through our fears.

Sometimes the dream world into which we would escape is the world of imagination, but there is danger in remaining there in place of coming back to enact what we envision. Creativity only bears fruit when we put it into action in the world.

If we delay making decisions and taking the necessary steps to make our dreams a reality, we may believe that we are keeping all our options open. But is this really so? Or are we succumbing to self-doubt or a concern that we do not have what it takes to succeed? If we refrain from decisive action, then it may be time to consider whether our lack of action is really a decision to abandon our dream. Will we act before the sand in the hourglass runs down?

Fear can be a warning of danger we need to avoid, but fear that is not dealt with can paralyze us when we ought to keep moving forward. Courage does not mean an absence of fear; rather, it is that which allows us to keep moving forward in the face of fear. Odysseus demonstrates in this episode that he has the courage to face his fears and to keep moving toward his goal.

SELF-WORTH AND SENSITIVITY TO OTHERS

For some of us, fear can be all-pervading, overwhelming—whether it is fear of disapproval, of rejection, of not getting a job, not being liked, fear of what we do not understand, and so on, all the way to the fear of death. How do we overcome it?

Fear comes from an absence of self-confidence, a lack of self-worth. The way to displacing it is to develop confidence in our inner worth. When we are not in balance physically, we are not at our strongest. The same principle applies to our inner world. If we are not in balance in our inner being, we will not be as confident as we can be; and a lack of self-worth provides a breeding ground for fear. We fear because we feel weak or unclear about what to do. To remedy this, to gain more balance, we will need to strengthen the weaker elements in our system, in our outlook and attitude to life. When we face our fear by looking inside with courage to discover what it is that we are afraid of, we will also discover what steps we can take to alleviate the source of fear.

Another related challenge in this trial with the Lotus Eaters is a tendency to be easily influenced by others.

If we are sensitive, intuitive and compassionate but not on guard when we are tested on this point of self-mastery, we may feel overpowered by the actions and feelings of others, especially discordant ones, and want to withdraw. Withdrawal can take many forms, including substance abuse, overeating, passivity, laziness, daydreaming, procrastination, addiction to sex or movies or romance novels, a feeling of victimization or despondency—anything that takes our mind off the challenges at hand.

Leading a balanced life includes taking care of our health and making time for recreation. After we have given our all to a cause, a period of rest may be necessary to rejuvenate us and prepare us for our next round of service. Odysseus and his men need rejuvenation. But an important distinction exists between balanced, healthy recreation and escapism, or slipping into a dream world.

Chronic escapism can lead to what I call "sweet death." Think of those blissful but oblivious crew members who ate the honey-sweet lotus and promptly forgot their home. In a sense, "sweet death" is like the condition induced by the lotus—a blissful indolence that leads us to believe that all is well while in truth our lack of decisive action is causing us to forsake our goals. In this manner, "sweet death" would steal our cherished dreams while we remain unaware that our hope for realizing them is fading. This is a dangerous state of mind.

When we have self-mastery, we are able to be sensitive to others yet we are also able to act decisively according to our own needs. We have the sensitivity to know when it is safe to rest and when we must dig deep, draw forth our inner resources, and continue to push forward for a worthy purpose. As the firm and decisive actions of Odysseus demonstrate in this episode, we will keep our head clear, assess our options, prioritize our desires, and hold firmly to our goals.

◉ ANCHORING YOUR INSIGHTS ◉

Two o'Clock Line

⟨ TESTS OF SELF-MASTERY ⟩

STRENGTHS	WEAKNESSES
self-mastery; walks through the fear	fear, doubt, self-doubt
mystical, spiritual, artistic, imaginative, dramatic	escapist, impractical, not grounded in practical life
idealistic, optimistic; wants to do the "right" thing	easily influenced, indecisive, emotionally up and down
kindly, gentle, unassuming but has sense of self-worth	passive, lacking willpower, low self-confidence
self-sacrificing, enduring, compassionate	exhausted, stubborn, emotional, self-pitying
intuitive; sensitive to pain, thoughts, feelings of others	impressionable; has overactive imagination

WHO AM I?
TWO O'CLOCK LINE: SELF-MASTERY

Take a moment to think about self-mastery in your life. Reflect on the chart of strengths and weaknesses and use it to evaluate your expressions of self-mastery. Later in this chapter, you will have an opportunity to map your strategy for turning weaknesses into strengths.

What are my greatest strengths in relation to self-mastery?

_____
_____
_____

What are my greatest weaknesses, especially forms of escapism, in relation to self-mastery?

_____
_____
_____

Thus far in my life, how have I handled challenges involving aspects of self-mastery? Would I handle any of those situations differently now? How?

_____
_____
_____

What can I learn about myself and self-mastery from Odysseus' and his crew's experience?

_____
_____
_____

WINNING STRATEGIES
TWO O'CLOCK LINE: SELF-MASTERY

KEEP THE VISION. Having a strong sense of your mission in life will keep you afloat above fears, doubts and other obstacles that may assail you on your path through life. Many people feel fear but do not know where the fear is coming from.

Beat fear and doubt by developing a strong vision and following through with a practical action plan.

ANCHOR YOURSELF. If you are not clear about your mission in life, you can end up living someone else's dream. When you notice yourself drifting on the seas, being pulled this way and that, you need something to anchor you until you can sail onward without veering off course. What anchors you? Your first and ultimate anchor is within you, your higher self. You also have anchors in the world.

Identify your anchor and use it when needed, and one day you will see a shining beacon indicating that you are in sight of your goal.

BUILD AND MAINTAIN HEALTHY BOUNDARIES. Intuition and sensitivity are positive attributes, but to keep yourself in balance you must be on guard not to let yourself be swayed easily by others. Empathy for others is a positive quality when it is tempered by healthy boundaries.

Healthy boundaries are like a fortress; they protect you from the penetration of unwanted energies.

Learn the difference between compassion and sympathy. Sympathy pulls people down by reinforcing the human condition. Compassion uplifts both giver and receiver.

The way to help others is to remain where you are and uplift them through compassion.

COME OUT OF YOUR DREAM WORLD. We may be tempted to use our imagination as a *substitute* for action rather than as a precursor to action. Wallowing in illusion or in an overactive imagination can keep you from reaching your goals. If you don't intend to complete a task, there is no point in starting it.

Finishing the important tasks you set for yourself before moving on to other activities will keep you on track to reaching your goals.

TRANSFORM DISCOURAGEMENT INTO COURAGE. Think of courage (or *coeur-age*) as the coming of age of the heart (*coeur* in French). Courage is the development of the love and wisdom of the heart that emboldens you to take the action that is right, honorable and necessary, even if it is temporarily uncomfortable. It is the antidote to fear. To be discouraged is to be deprived of courage or confidence.

Transform discouragement into the courage that will take you through life's challenges.

WHERE AM I GOING?
TWO O'CLOCK LINE: SELF-MASTERY

As you reflect on the following, you may find it helpful to review the various aspects of self-mastery in the chart on p. 70 and "The Stuff Heroes Are Made Of" on pp. 4–5, as well as the Winning Strategies. Using the questions below, map out a strategy to apply the insights you've gained.

In the tests of self-mastery presented by my current life circumstances, how can I use my strengths constructively?

_____

_____

_____

How can I turn any weakness I may have into an expression of self-mastery that I can claim as a new strength?

_____

_____

_____

Where can I use sensitivity and imagination to make concrete progress in my life?

_____

_____

_____

What are my anchors? How can I regain command of my attention from any habits of escapism to focus on achieving my goals?

_____

_____

_____

IF YOU HAVE BUILT CASTLES IN THE AIR,
YOUR WORK NEED NOT BE LOST; THAT IS
WHERE THEY SHOULD BE. NOW PUT THE
FOUNDATIONS UNDER THEM.

HENRY DAVID THOREAU

Three o'Clock Line

FULCRUM OF CONTROL

FOLLOWING
THE ROUTE OF
ODYSSEUS

Three o'Clock Line

FULCRUM OF CONTROL

So headstrong—why? Why rile the beast again?
ODYSSEUS' MEN

Odysseus and his crew stop next at the land of the one-eyed giants known as the Cyclopes. Odysseus tells us that each of the Cyclopes "dwells in his own mountain cave dealing out rough justice to wife and child, indifferent to what the others do." (IX:113–115) The men feast on what they find there, but Odysseus is not satisfied with food. He is curious. With twelve of his men, he decides to explore further.

They enter the wide, empty cavern of the Cyclops Polyphemus. The men beg Odysseus to take some of the goats and cheese they find there and leave quickly. Odysseus refuses to listen. At his direction, they build a fire, offer a sacrifice, and then help themselves to cheese.

Polyphemus eventually returns for the night. Odysseus describes him as "a monstrous wonder made to behold, not like a man...but more like a wooded peak of the high mountains...." The Cyclops drives the sheep inside and then sets a massive stone slab across the cavern entrance. Odysseus and his men are trapped inside with the giant. The stone, Odysseus says, is "a massive thing; no twenty-two of the best four-wheeled wagons could have taken that weight off the ground and carried it, such a piece of sky-towering cliff that was he set over his gateway." (IX:190–192, 241–244)

In those days it was the custom to honor strangers with hospitality gifts, and Odysseus tries to compel the Cyclops to offer him gifts. But the Cyclops mocks him: "You are a simple fool...when you tell me to avoid the wrath of the gods or fear them. The Cyclopes do not concern themselves over Zeus...nor any of the rest of the

Odysseus and his men drive a spike through the Cyclops' single eye, blinding him.

blessed gods, since we are far better than they." (IX:273–277) He snatches up two of Odysseus' men and eats them before going to sleep.

The next morning Polyphemus eats another two men. Then he lets his sheep out. He repositions the massive stone slab over the cave opening in order to prevent an escape, then goes off to tend his herds. While he is away, the crafty Odysseus hatches a plot. He sharpens a staff he finds in the cave and hides it.

That night, after the Cyclops feasts on two more men, Odysseus offers him a potent, undiluted wine. Polyphemus drinks enough to affect his brain. He asks Odysseus what his name is and Odysseus answers shrewdly, "Nobody is my name." (IX:366) The giant falls into a drunken stupor and slumber. Odysseus and his men drive the spike into the embers and ram its hot point through the Cyclops' single eye, blinding him. Polyphemus bellows and pulls out the spike.

His fellow Cyclopes, hearing his cries, gather around the outside of the sealed cave and ask: "What ails you?" He roars back, "Nobody is killing me by force or treachery." (IX:403–404; IX:408) "If you're alone," they respond, "and nobody's trying to overpower you now— look, it must be a plague sent here by mighty Zeus and there's no escape from *that*. You'd better pray to your father, Lord Poseidon." Odysseus' plan having succeeded thus far, he says, "They lumbered off, but laughter filled my heart to think how nobody's name—my great cunning stroke—had duped them one and all." (IX:410–414)

The following morning the men are able to escape from the cave by another ingenious trick. Odysseus ties

Odysseus taunts the Cyclops. Enraged, Polyphemus breaks off a hilltop and heaves it in the direction of their boat.

each man underneath three rams. As the blind Cyclops lets the rams out of the cave he strokes each one but never detects the men underneath them. The men dash to the ship and pull away from the shore. But instead of slipping silently away, Odysseus rashly shouts to the Cyclops: "How do you like the beating that we gave you, you damned cannibal? Eater of guests under your roof! Zeus and the gods have paid you!" (IX:475–479)

This taunt enrages Polyphemus. He breaks off a hilltop and heaves it in the direction of their boat, creating a wave that washes them back to shore. Odysseus' men again offer good advice to their impetuous leader. They protest, "Captain! Why bait the beast again? Let him alone!" But Odysseus ignores them, and in his anger and pride he shouts: "Cyclops, if ever mortal man inquire how you were put to shame and blinded, tell him Odysseus, raider of cities, took your eye: Laertes' son, whose home's on Ithaca!" (IX:494, 502–505)

Polyphemus shifts tactics. He asks Odysseus to come back and promises that he will treat him well. But Odysseus replies: "If I could take your life I would...and hurl you down to hell!" (IX:523–524) Fateful words. The repercussions of this curse descend swiftly.

Polyphemus, now thoroughly enraged, curses Odysseus. The Cyclops prays to his father, Poseidon: "Grant that Odysseus, raider of cities, never see his home.... Should destiny intend that he shall see his roof again among his family in his father land, far be that day, and dark the years between. Let him lose all companions, and return under strange sail to bitter days at home." (IX:530–535)

At last, Odysseus and his crew row swiftly away from the danger, grieving for their lost companions. They rejoin the other ships.

LIFE REFLECTS THE INNER STRUGGLE

In his encounter with the Cyclops, Odysseus defends his ego. By doing so he puts himself and his crew at great risk. Half of the men he brings into this encounter do not survive it.

The Cyclops episode graphically shows us that the inner foes we struggle with are reflected in those we encounter in life. Odysseus, brave and crafty warrior that he is, is also arrogant. In this trial Odysseus is seeing his own giant-size ego reflected in the Cyclops. Symbolically,

Polyphemus is the embodiment of his own arrogant inner beast. Odysseus' insistence on lingering in the giant's cave results in the death of six men. And even then, after he and his remaining crew members barely escape the giant's clutching hands, Odysseus still does not surrender his ego. He nearly gets himself and the rest of his men killed by reacting to what he perceives to be an insult to his honor.

It takes a certain amount of self-control to endure insults without reacting. If, for example, Odysseus had followed the advice of his men, who in this instance represent the voice of caution, self-control and staying focused on the goal, he would have beat a fast retreat. Instead he hurls insults at the Cyclops and then, again ignoring the voice of reason, gives in to an overwhelming desire to flaunt his ego by revealing his identity. "It is Odysseus who blinded you!" he shouts. This act of pride leaves him utterly vulnerable, because the Cyclops would never have been able to curse Odysseus effectively if Odysseus had not told him his name. As a result of Odysseus' rash egotism, Polyphemus is able to call upon his father, Poseidon, to avenge him against Odysseus, son of Laertes. Poseidon plagues Odysseus' journey for years to come.

Odysseus is also tested in this trial on self-expression, which can also be seen as an aspect of self-control. Odysseus asserts his identity at great cost. He shows no sense of humility and he tempts the fates for no good reason. Despite the fact that Odysseus' greatest desire is to go home to his beloved Ithaca and to his beloved wife and son, he lets pride and arrogance entangle him in a web of trouble.

Some commentators say that Odysseus had to state his identity to the Cyclops, because a hero will never relinquish his identity. But as I see it, the Cyclops episode brings to the fore one of the primary lessons Odysseus must learn during his long and arduous odyssey. It is a test we all face, the test of humility.

THE VULNERABILITY OF THE EGO

To his credit, Odysseus, by his willingness to take action, devises an effective plan that allows him and his men to escape from the Cyclops. On the other hand, he falls into the trap of pride, of being headstrong, and of not heeding the sound advice of his crew. His curiosity entices him to impulsively explore the land of the Cyclops. There is nothing wrong with a little curiosity or impulsiveness in the right circumstances. But in this case, Odysseus' disregard of caution and reckless indulgence of his curiosity and ego reveal a lack of self-control. He temporarily lets his goal of getting back home take a back seat and it nearly costs him his life. Odysseus ignores the needs and desires of his men, then pits his wits and ego against the giant Cyclops. By so doing he puts the entire mission at risk.

If we are not in control of ourselves, we are susceptible to becoming combative. When we defend our ego, we make ourselves vulnerable. The bigger the ego, the greater the vulnerability. We never really win when we struggle for the mere sake of a struggle, just for the sake of arguing, of being "right," of defeating someone or putting someone down. Although we may think we win, we never really do.

The human ego is simply not defensible. Neither is the ego a good defender. The more we use the ego as our defender, the greater our vulnerability becomes. Rather than trusting in our ego to defend us, our safety lies in defending the position of our higher self as the guiding force within us. When we remain in the consciousness of our higher self, we will not enter into the lower levels of pride and the human consciousness. Our higher consciousness can defeat any lesser aspect of consciousness, whether we have struggled with it for decades or only recently.

Do we really have to be aggressive to get what we want? In a word, no. But sometimes we fall into the trap of being aggressive instead of centering in the heart. Aggression is unnecessary. Our higher self is within us; therefore, we do not need to stoop to aggression to get what we want. We can look at each trial, its archetypal quality, its positive and negative aspects, and be able to say the same thing: We do not need to express any negative trait, because our higher self is within us.

What causes us to be defensive? Is it because we feel the need to defend a wounded ego? Have we identified with that ego rather than with our higher self? We do not have to be impulsive because our higher self will direct us, increment by increment, through every step we must take to get on the right track and stay on it. Understanding this will bring us great healing if we truly accept it.

WEIGHING THE ADVICE OF OTHERS

Another test Odysseus faces with regard to self-control is the test whether to heed or reject the advice of others. Several times in his battle with his giant ego, Odysseus refuses to heed the wise counsel of his crew. He is so headstrong that he does not even reflect on what the others say or need. In order for our interactions with others to succeed, we need to think first about what impact our actions will have on them and whether our actions will benefit them. As this episode with the Cyclops demonstrates, if everything we do is all about us and what we want, and not about anyone else, it is time to stop and think.

If we blindly follow the advice of others, we will not develop the discrimination it takes to forge our victories in life. We can, however, learn from the wisdom, experience and intuition of others. Instead of rejecting their advice outright or blindly accepting it, we can listen politely and openly to what they say and then go within to discern what is right for us. If their advice is sound, we can determine how best to apply it to our situation.

Every challenge Odysseus faces is applicable to us today, to our own odyssey. Falling into an ego trap, as Odysseus does in this episode with the Cyclops, could be anyone's undoing. We all do fine when things are going well. Problems arise when we get overly emotional about things. When we are so deeply emotional that we lose self-control, we readily forget, at least temporarily, to battle the negative tendencies that we have stirred up. Emotions rile the beast in us. The challenge, as always, is to choose to amplify love within our heart. Love is the quality that will bring us back to center, back to what really matters. When we feel love overflowing within us, we do not feel a need to defend the ego, to attack anyone, or to ignore the needs of others.

A DETERMINED PLAN TO SUCCEED

Among Odysseus' enduring traits is his refusal to accept defeat or be stopped by setbacks. He keeps charging ahead. When kept in balance through good self-control, these are strengths that can get the wheel of our mission spinning and keep it spinning. But when we can see the handwriting on the wall, as in this encounter with the Cyclops, it does not serve us to keep charging forward. Sometimes the better part of wisdom is to call a time-out in order to strategize our next steps and refine a plan to secure our victory.

Most of us are not battling physical monsters and man-eating giants. But many of us struggle with negative traits that are like man-eaters. They slowly eat away at our self-esteem and our sense of who we are and where we are going in life. These harmful patterns can slow us down or even bring us to a standstill, and if we ignore them they may ultimately prevent us from fulfilling those things that are dearest to us.

Let us say, for an example, that we have a negative trait that we have not really wrestled with. Then one day we get determined and say, "I am simply not going to do this anymore!" Like making a New Year's resolution, we start out with a strong resolve. Some of us follow through to victory on those resolutions. But we may just get distracted from our goal and fall short here and there. Pretty soon we may let our determination slide altogether. We may even forget why we were so set on overcoming that particular trait.

Setting a timetable for overcoming that trait can be just the strategy we need to put an end to it once and for all. We can say, "By [name a realistic date], I will have replaced [name a weakness or negative trait] with [name a strength or positive trait that is its opposite or that you want to replace it with]." We can set that date for a day or a month or six months from now. We have to know ourselves and be realistic about what we can achieve, but when we set a timetable for overcoming a specific trait and give ourselves a clear goal to strive for, we are likely to show a greater determination to accomplish it.

What do we do if we fall back into a negative trait or attitude that we are determined to overcome? Get back up and start over again! Making mistakes is not what causes us to fail. It is making the same mistake over and over and not getting to the root of why we are doing it that can be our undoing. Being unwilling to learn from our mistakes and insisting instead on human perfection is a form of pride.

Think back to the hallmarks of a hero (pp. 4–5). A hero is not afraid to make a mistake, and when he does, he bounces back from it. He learns from his mistakes and does not dwell on the past. Odysseus, in spite of the mistakes he makes, is still sailing toward home. *And he will make it.* If we repeatedly condemn ourselves for our mistakes, we will feel unworthy to succeed. But if we pick ourselves up and start over when we make a mistake, we will slowly but surely build a positive momentum on overcoming.

PRIDE WEARS MANY COSTUMES

Pride comes wrapped in many costumes, a whole range of attitudes. Tests of pride come regularly and sometimes they come when we least expect them. How can we cope with our ego? We can look to the wisdom within us and hand over control of a situation to our higher self, which is where genuine self-control comes from. Then we can open the door to possibilities we never thought of before. Truly, it is the sense of struggle that makes the struggle.

Overconcern and anxiety can function like blinders, narrowing our view to where we cannot see all the options. In fact, we may be looking for answers in all the wrong places. When we are open to another way of seeing things, then our inner knowing can bring the highest solution to us. My late husband and teacher, Mark L. Prophet, used to say we are never going to find the answer we are looking for outside of ourselves. "It's in yourself," he said. "That's where the search begins. We can discover a gold mine of consciousness within.... And when we find that consciousness, we will have a new appreciation of our net worth. You don't find your net worth on a financial statement; you find it inside of you."

The consciousness of our lesser self identifies with pride, control, the sense of power, and so forth. Thus, in order to pass the tests of ego and self-control, we need to raise our consciousness to the level of our higher self.

WE ARE BIGGER THAN THAT

When we lack a strong connection to our higher self, we are more likely to feel insulted or offended by what other people say or do to us. The part of us that gets insulted is the ego, the same part that is easily impressed. These are opposite sides of the same coin. It is the ego that is easily impressed and the ego that feels insulted. When we are centered in our higher self, we are neither insulted nor impressed.

So where do we get lost? How is it that we slip into our ego so fast that we are not even aware of it? And how can we get back to center and stay centered in our higher self?

To step out from behind the ego, from thinking the ego is our defender, we need to live in the presence and awareness of our higher self, the loving adult within us that cares for us. That is where we have to position ourselves.

If we find ourselves reacting to others, this is a signal to us that in that moment we are not centered in our higher self. When we act from our lesser self, we can at times feel so separate from others. We may feel isolated and apart from every other individual rather than feeling our interconnectedness. But we can choose mindfully to return to center. When we are centered and perfectly balanced, we can have a profound experience in quiet moments of feeling a tremendous merging, through love, with all life.

☽ ANCHORING YOUR INSIGHTS ☾

Three o'Clock Line

TESTS OF SELF-CONTROL

STRENGTHS	WEAKNESSES
self-control, humble self-leadership	pride, tendency to anger; reactionary
courageous; refuses to accept defeat	headstrong, rash; fights unnecessary battles
enthusiastic, energetic, highly motivated	aggressive, impatient, impulsive, overly forceful
seeks to be first and best as the striving of the higher self	overly competitive, does not listen to others; big ego
pioneering, independent, original	self-centered; seeks admiration or praise
self-expressive, self-assertive, direct	opinionated, argumentative

WHO AM I?
THREE O'CLOCK LINE: SELF-CONTROL

Take a moment to think about self-control in your life. Reflect on the chart of strengths and weaknesses and use it to evaluate your expressions of self-control. Later in this chapter, you will have an opportunity to map your strategy for turning weaknesses into strengths.

What are my greatest strengths in relation to self-control?

_____
_____
_____

What are my greatest weaknesses in relation to self-control? Do I have a Cyclops lurking somewhere within me?

_____
_____
_____

Thus far in my life, how have I handled challenges involving aspects of self-control and ego? Would I handle any of those situations differently now? How?

_____
_____
_____

What can I learn about myself and self-control from Odysseus' experience?

_____
_____
_____

Winning Strategies
THREE O'CLOCK LINE: SELF-CONTROL

DO NOT TAKE THINGS PERSONALLY. BE AN OB-SERVER. The human ego gets defensive when it meets with resistance. When we take other people's actions personally, we tend to fight battles that do not have to be fought.

A key to self-control is detachment. If you find yourself getting worked up over something, detach from the outer circumstances. Anchor yourself in a calm place within your heart. From that secure vantage, observe the passing scene with detachment rather than participating in it like a cork bobbing on the waves. You cannot control the behavior of others but you can control your reaction to it. When you lose self-control, you set yourself back.

Resolve underlying issues and tether yourself to your real self-worth, which comes from the higher aspects of your being. Then you will no longer be buffeted by outer circumstances.

UNEARTH AND RESOLVE POCKETS OF HIDDEN ANGER AND HURT. Feelings of anger and hurt are not something many of us like to take a look at. However, if you continually suppress these feelings instead of resolving their underlying cause, you will be stopping up the flow of energy that could be redirected into other things. In addition, until you resolve these issues you may be suffering and causing others to suffer, especially when that energy finally erupts.

Beneath anger there is usually hurt. Resolve the underlying cause and free your energy.

FOCUS ON THE NEEDS OF OTHERS AND ON THE CONSEQUENCES OF YOUR ACTIONS. If we do not balance our needs with those of others, we may become headstrong in carrying out our personal agenda. If you find yourself in this situation, consciously focus on others and think about the consequences of your actions both for yourself and for them. Doing so can prevent you from directing your enthusiasm into a blunder.

When our focus is exclusively on ourselves, the energy of the heart can become concave (inward-directed) rather than convex (outward-directed).

Develop sensitivity to the needs of others.

MAKE ROOM FOR YOUR HIGHER SELF. So long as we are filled with a sense of self-importance, our petty concerns and our need for recognition (as Odysseus was in the episode with the Cyclops), we have no room to be filled with the various aspects of our higher self. The container can only hold so much.

Empty yourself of the elements of your lesser self to make room for the elements of your higher self.

LET LOVE TRANSFORM EVERY NEGATIVE INTO A POSITIVE EXPRESSION. Mary Baker Eddy said, "Divine Love always has met and always will meet every human need." Those who allow love to dwell within them will—without fear, without sense of loss—replace the human ego with the consciousness of the higher self. Love is the key.

When you take the first tentative steps to letting go of the human ego, you may at first feel a vacancy. This feeling of emptiness comes from the absence of something familiar.

Let love fill the vacuum. Love can transmute every negative, from beginning to end, into a positive expression.

WHERE AM I GOING?

THREE O'CLOCK LINE: SELF-CONTROL

As you reflect on the following questions, you may find it helpful to review the various aspects of self-control in the chart on p. 92 and "The Stuff Heroes Are Made Of" on pp. 4–5, as well as the Winning Strategies. Using the questions below, map out a strategy to apply the insights you've gained.

In the tests of self-control presented by my current life circumstances, how can I use my strengths constructively?

_____

_____

How can I turn any weakness I may have into an expression of self-control that I can claim as a new strength? What realistic timeline can I set to do this?

_____

_____

_____

What are some ways that I can cultivate a sense of the interconnectedness of life that takes me beyond my ego?

_____

_____

_____

Is there a situation in my life where I need to be courageous and charge ahead? How can I do that while maintaining an awareness of my impact on other people?

_____

_____

_____

SELF-REVERENCE, SELF-KNOWLEDGE,
SELF-CONTROL—THESE THREE ALONE LEAD
LIFE TO SOVEREIGN POWER.

ALFRED, LORD TENNYSON

Four o'Clock Line

KEEPING THE GOAL IN SIGHT

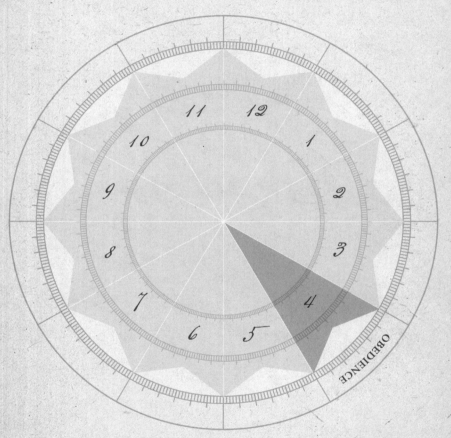

Four o'Clock Line

KEEPING THE GOAL IN SIGHT

*Aiolos set the West Wind free to blow us on
our way.... But his plan was bound to fail, yes, our
own reckless folly swept us on to ruin.*
ODYSSEUS

After their escape from the land of the Cyclopes, Odysseus and his men make their next stop at Aiolia Island, where the wind king, Aiolos, hosts them. Odysseus spends a month with Aiolos and his family. They entertain him with daily feasts while he regales them with tales of Troy.

When Odysseus and his men are ready to sail, Aiolos gives him a parting gift, a sturdy ox skin filled with all the winds but one. The wind king stows the bag in the hollow of Odysseus' ship, tying it securely with a silver cord so that not even a breath of contrary wind can escape to hinder their arrival at Ithaca. He leaves the west wind free to blow Odysseus and his crew safely home. Odysseus knows the contents of the bag but does not share this knowledge with his crew.

Aiolos leaves the west wind free to blow Odysseus and his crew safely home.

For nine days and nine nights, a steady west wind drives the ships homeward. During this entire time Odysseus remains awake, constantly directing the course of his ship. He is determined that no delay will occur.

On the tenth day the ships sail within sight of Ithaca—so close they can see people tending their fires. With his goal in sight, Odysseus, weary to the bone, falls into a deep slumber. While he lies sleeping, his companions speculate about the contents of the gift bag from the wind king, saying one to the other:

See now, this man is loved by everybody and favored by all, whenever he visits anyone's land and city, and is bringing home with him handsome treasures taken from the plunder of Troy, while we, who have gone through

everything he has on the same venture, come home with
our hands empty. Now too Aiolos in favor of friendship
has given him all these goods. Let us quickly look inside
and see what is in there, and how much silver and gold
this bag contains inside it. (X:38–45)

"The evil counsel of my companions prevailed," says Odysseus, "and they opened the bag." (X:46–47) The storm winds burst out of the bag, roaring into heavy squalls that sweep them back and away from their homeland.

Odysseus contemplates suicide: "Then I waking pondered deeply in my own blameless spirit, whether to throw myself over the side and die in the open water, or wait it out in silence and still be one of the living." He determines to endure. "And hiding my face I lay down in the ship, while all were carried on the evil blast of the storm-wind back to the Aiolian island, with my friends grieving." (X:49–52, 53–55)

Odysseus pleads with Aiolos to help him home again. Aiolos refuses. He says he will not help a man whom the gods evidently detest. "Groan as I did," Odysseus says, "his curses drove me from his halls and from there we pulled away with heavy hearts, with the crews' spirit broken under the oars' labor, thanks to our own folly...no favoring wind in sight." (X:76–79)

Odysseus and his companions sail for six days and six nights without stopping. On the seventh day, they reach the land of the Laistrygones, where man-eating giants destroy eleven of his twelve ships along with their crew. Odysseus' ship is spared only because it is anchored apart from the others, outside the harbor.

The storm winds, released by Odysseus' men, burst out of the bag and roar into heavy squalls.

SELF-WORTH IS OF MORE VALUE THAN TREASURE

In this trial, Odysseus and his men are tested on the archetypal quality of obedience. Speaking of their failure to reach Ithaca after coming within sight of it, Odysseus admits, "We were ruined by our own folly." (X:27)

Odysseus' crew members signal rebellion through their disobedience. Through jealousy and a lust for material goods, the men bring disaster upon themselves. Right when they are in sight of their goal, they let themselves be distracted by greed. They believe that Odysseus is more favored than they are and it peeves them. They also think that having a share in the treasure will make them feel better about themselves.

Odysseus' men also fare poorly in another test that is related to obedience, the test of loyalty. The men do not remain steadfast in their loyalty to Odysseus. He has been their captain through thick and thin for over ten years, yet they let their jealousy of him take over. Because they do not trust him to deal fairly and generously with them, they resent that he is well liked and is treated generously by others. In essence, they say: "Odysseus is welcome everywhere. He's returning home with lots of treasures. But we're empty-handed." Not trusting that Odysseus will reward them justly for their years of loyalty and for a job well done, they attempt to take their own reward by stealing it.

This attitude, assuming that they will get nothing unless they seize it for themselves, indicates low self-esteem. In consequence they receive an opportunity to learn the hard way that those who take their own rewards leave no room for others to reward them and they may end up empty-handed.

In this episode with the bag of winds, we see that greed and rebellion will take us far off course. We also see that having a sense of self-worth is more valuable than all the treasure in the world.

The desire for material goods can be a trap whereby we feel a strong urge to accumulate goods so we can have the physical things we believe we need to feel good about ourselves or to express ourselves. While this can lead us to skillfully manage our resources, it can also lead to excessive materialism and an enmeshment in things. The key is to treat possessions not as an end in themselves but as a vehicle for accomplishing goals.

LOYALTY AND BEING ON GUARD

Odysseus has not mastered the test of loyalty either. In this episode he displays mistrust for the very men who have served under his command for more than a decade. Through his possessiveness of the bag of winds and his failure to share information vital to the success of the journey, Odysseus fuels his crew members' temptation to rebel.

If Odysseus had told his men the contents of the ox skin bag, would they still have been tempted to open it? If he had trusted them to man the sails and keep the ship on course, would they have merited his trust by discharging their duties faithfully? These questions are impossible to answer but they give us pause for self-reflection.

Alternatively, Odysseus might have commanded his men to keep him awake during those final moments of the journey so that he did not succumb to sleep. But again, would they have done so? Or would their greed and curiosity have gotten the better of them? We cannot say. But we do know that Odysseus, by keeping essential knowledge and all the responsibility to himself, comes within sight of his goal only to watch it slip away at the last moment.

In short, at least in this episode, Odysseus and his men do not act with mutual trust and loyalty. We see these patterns sometimes in groups and in the workplace when leaders do not share vital information with their team. When team leaders do not show trust for those who work under them, the entire team is vulnerable to falling apart. Conversely, when team members don't trust the leader to deal fairly with them, currents of resentment and disloyalty begin to flow and communication can break down rapidly.

Falling asleep within sight of a goal can represent quitting work too soon on a project. In some cases, this can result in serious consequences. That extra effort might just be all we need to secure a contract, to achieve a new level of self-mastery or to master a skill, or to make a difference in whether a product we are about to put on the market is safe or reliable.

Falling asleep is also symbolic of being off guard. In contrast, being awake symbolizes being centered in reality and being unfettered by illusions, including the illusion that material possessions will bring us fulfillment.

OBEDIENCE TO INNER AND OUTER GUIDANCE

In this trial with the bag of winds, we see that being stubborn or possessive, as Odysseus was, or being disobedient or rebellious, as his men were, can have lasting repercussions. If we are consistently rebellious or stubborn, we may confuse these traits with independence. Repeatedly defying authority or the law, even in small ways, or thinking we can make an exception "just this once," such as exceeding the speed limit or cheating on an exam, then farther along the road we may become ensnared in more serious forms of rebellion or in a dangerous situation.

Obedience is not necessarily to an external authority. Obedience means following our intuition, the inner direction and guidance we receive from our higher self. At times this inner prompting may come as a warning which, if we follow it, will protect us from harm. Recall that after the raid on the Kikonians, Odysseus felt a strong urge to leave Ismaros quickly rather than to remain on the beach feasting.

No doubt we have all had the experience of having an intuition about something but ignoring it, and then realizing a short while later that we should have followed it. Maybe it would have saved us some extra steps or helped us to connect with a friend. If we treat these promptings as tests from our higher self and follow them with awareness, we will learn to trust our intuition. Sometimes the reason we receive a prompting may not be obvious to us except in retrospect. This personal story serves as an example:

One day when I was in college, as I was leaving my apartment, I felt an inner prompting to put on a thick winter coat and gloves. That did not make sense to me, because it was springtime in Boston and the day seemed likely to be a warm one. I felt the prompting again, so I put on my heavy winter coat. But I really could not see any reason to put on my winter gloves so I didn't. Then, because I was slightly late for school, I started walking between cars that were stopped in the morning traffic. The next thing I knew, along came a fast-moving bicycle and we bumped right into each other. I fell to the pavement. The heavy coat padded my fall and protected me from injury everywhere except to my bare hands.

This incident taught me the importance of listening to my inner voice even when it seems nonsensical, like wearing a heavy winter coat on a warm day. Of course it would be inappropriate to do something that seems dangerous, and we still have to use common sense, because sometimes a prompting might stem from an unresolved emotional issue and not from our inner wisdom. That said, we can always test an assignment or intuition that we believe is from our higher self by reflecting on its parameters and assessing its safety in the context of the specific situation.

Obedience also includes disciplines such as being on time, meeting commitments, doing a job well, and being dependable. Being on time even in small matters helps us develop a discipline that will keep us on schedule in our life.

In our soul's odyssey, we all have recourse to the wisdom and guidance of our higher self to help us identify our destiny, create a practical action plan for achieving it, and fine-tune our plan as we proceed. Nonetheless, we still have to make a conscious commitment to be obedient to our inner guidance and to stay with our vision until it comes to fruition.

Four o'Clock Line

TESTS OF OBEDIENCE

STRENGTHS	WEAKNESSES
loyal, self-disciplined, obedient	disloyal, defiant, rebellious; takes exception to rules
trustworthy, reliable; waits for reward	jealous, possessive, needy of security or reward
listens to intuition, inner calling	ignores inner guidance
determined, strong-willed, persevering, persistent	stubborn, rigid
self-worth comes from within; values inner self	materialistic, image-conscious; judges worth by possessions
deliberate, slow to anger, quiet	over-blown anger once it happens

WHO AM I?
FOUR O'CLOCK LINE: OBEDIENCE

Take a moment to think about obedience in your life. Reflect on the chart of strengths and weaknesses and use it to evaluate your expressions of obedience. Later in this chapter, you will have an opportunity to map your strategy for turning weaknesses into strengths.

What are my greatest strengths in relation to obedience?

_____

_____

_____

What are my greatest weaknesses in relation to obedience?

_____

_____

_____

Thus far in my life, how have I handled challenges involving aspects of obedience? Have I ever let the wrong winds that took me away from my goals out of the bag? Would I handle any of those situations differently now? How?

_____

_____

_____

What can I learn about myself and obedience from Odysseus' experience?

_____

_____

_____

WINNING STRATEGIES
FOUR O'CLOCK LINE: OBEDIENCE

CHERISH AND VALUE YOUR SOUL FOR WHO YOU REALLY ARE. Many people struggle with issues of self-image and self-worth. You may compensate by filling yourself up with food and things that give temporary comfort or by acquiring things that enhance your image, such as money, power, status, material possessions. But all the treasure in the world cannot displace insecurity.

Envision your soul, or your inner child, as joyful and pure, innocent and beautiful, embraced by your higher self, your wise and loving inner adult. Find your treasure in your higher self.

Your core reality is love and your soul is worthy of love.

MAKE YOUR MATERIAL DESIRES SERVE YOUR MISSION. If your focus is primarily on acquiring things, you risk losing sight of your mission. The desire for possessions to adorn the ego could be the "lotus" that makes you forgetful of your real goals. On the other hand, material possessions can serve effectively as tools to assist you in the fulfillment of your mission.

Be aware of how you view and use possessions and what your relationship is to them.

REPLACE REBELLION WITH RESPECTFUL COMMUNICATION AND LOYALTY. Sometimes rebellion is against the circumstances of life. This is really a rebellion against reaping what has been sown or against being tested by life. Rebellion can also take the form of rigidity or refusal to accept advice or correction from others, especially from those with some authority over us.

Obedience or loyalty to a manager or team leader

at work, for example, does not mean blind obedience no matter what. When you disagree with a manager, find a way to do it respectfully. You could say, for example, "May I give you some information that might assist you in your deliberations?"

Tact and respect will help to convey your point in a positive, helpful way.

PRACTICE OBEDIENCE TO YOUR HIGHER SELF. If you take issue with the word *obedience*, it may be because it conjures up authority figures or tyrants you have faced. But obedience is not a matter of looking to others to define you or allowing them to control or restrict you. If you want to become who you really are, be willing to deal with the circumstances of your life right now. To move beyond your current circumstances, practice listening to and acing upon the guidance of your higher self.

With one ear you can listen to the world. With the other ear you can be always listening for the voice of your higher self.

ANCHOR YOUR SOUL'S DESTINY. In the course of unfolding and anchoring your soul's destiny, life will test you in many ways. As you transform negative aspects into character strengths, you will eventually clear all that stands between you and your destiny. Along the way, your victories and your increasing mastery of each quality will serve as an anchor to keep you on track.

Visualize anchoring yourselves to whatever level of attainment or self-mastery you currently have relating to a particular quality. That is the best you can do in this moment. A few hours from now or on another day, you will be able to do more. Drop anchor deep into that quality. Over time you will build a deeper and deeper sense of accomplishment, knowing what you can do today and knowing that you will be able to do more tomorrow and the next day, as long as you keep on keeping on.

Anchor yourself deeply in your current level of mastery of each quality you desire to have.

WHERE AM I GOING?

FOUR O'CLOCK LINE: OBEDIENCE

As you reflect on the following questions, you may find it helpful to review the various aspects of obedience in the chart on p. 110 and "The Stuff Heroes Are Made Of" on pp. 4–5, as well as the Winning Strategies. Using the questions below, map out a strategy to apply the insights you've gained.

In the tests of obedience presented by my current life circumstances, how can I use my strengths constructively?

_____
_____
_____

How can I turn any weakness I may have into an expression of obedience that I can claim as a new strength?

_____
_____
_____

What reminders can I give myself of my self-worth so that I'm not tempted to compensate with desires for things that take my attention off my real goals?

_____
_____
_____

Where in my life can I focus more on self-discipline, loyalty and obedience, whether to inner or outer guidance?

_____
_____
_____

CHARACTER IS FORMED IN THE STORMY
BILLOWS OF THE WORLD.

JOHANN WOLFGANG VON GOETHE

Five o'Clock Line

SWORD OF DISCERNMENT

Five o'Clock Line

SWORD OF DISCERNMENT

You have a mind in you no magic can enchant!
You must be Odysseus.
CIRCE

"**F**rom there we sailed on," says Odysseus, "glad to escape our death yet sick at heart for the dear companions we had lost." Odysseus and the crew of his remaining ship reach an island, "home of Circe the nymph with lovely braids, an awesome power too who can speak with human voice.... For two days and two nights we lay by there, eating our hearts out, bent with pain and bone-tired."(X:133–136, 142–143)

At dawn on the third day, Odysseus takes his sharp sword and spear and climbs a peak to a commanding view of the island. He cannot get his bearings, for he cannot tell "where the Sun who shines upon people rises, nor where he sets." (X:191–192) He spies smoke rising in the distance but decides to feed the men before exploring further. He returns to the ship carrying a great stag. He comforts each man in turn, rousing them all with kind words and the promise of a good meal. They spend the day "feasting on unlimited meat and sweet wine." (X:184)

The next morning, they draw lots to determine who will scout the island. Though "the inward heart in them was broken," (X:198) Eurylochos and an envoy of twenty-two men set off to explore.

> *Deep in the wooded glens they came on Circe's palace.... Mountain wolves and lions were roaming round the grounds.... But they wouldn't attack my men; they just came pawing up around them, fawning, swishing their long tails.... The men cringed in fear.... But still they paused at her doors...and deep inside they heard her singing, lifting her spellbinding voice as she glided back and forth at her great immortal loom, her enchanting web a shimmering glory only goddesses can weave.* (X:210, 212, 214–215, 219–224)

The voice of the goddess enthralls them and they call out to her. At Circe's invitation they enter her palace —all but Eurylochos, who suspects a snare. They sit on benches and chairs while she prepares a meal for them. She adds a drug to their wine that causes them to lose any desire or thought of their homeland. Then she strikes them with her wand and turns them into swine.

When it appears that all the men have vanished without a trace, Eurylochos runs back to the ship, filled with grief, and begs Odysseus to leave the island immediately to save the rest of them from doom.

Odysseus refuses to abandon his men and bravely

Circe offers Odysseus a cup of wine and prepares to thrust her wand at him.

sets off alone to rescue them. Along the way he meets the god Hermes, who explains that the men are holed up in Circe's pig pens. The god gives Odysseus an herb to eat, called *moly* by the gods, a "good medicine" that will protect him from Circe's spell. Hermes says, "This great herb with holy force will keep your mind and senses clear." (X:287, 288)

Hermes also tells Odysseus that when Circe comes at him with her long wand he must draw his sword and lunge at her as if raging to kill her. Hermes explains what will follow. He tells Odysseus not to refuse the goddess and then instructs him how to prevent further trickery.

Odysseus eats the powerful herb and then, with his heart beating hard, approaches Circe's palace. She invites him in and offers him a cup of the wine, to which she adds her drug. When her potion fails to enchant him, she thrusts her wand at him and says: "Down in the sty and snore among the rest!" (X:320)

Following Hermes' instruction, Odysseus draws his sharp sword and rushes Circe as if raging to kill her. Astounded, Circe falls to her knees and says: "Never has any other man withstood my potion, never.... You have a mind in *you* no magic can enchant! You must be Odysseus." She then invites Odysseus into her bed: "Put up

Odysseus rushes Circe as if raging to kill her.

your weapon in the sheath. We two shall mingle and make love upon our bed. So mutual trust may come of play and love." (X:327–330, 333–335)

Again following Hermes' instruction, Odysseus first makes Circe swear a great oath that she will do him and his shipmates no more harm. He also secures her agreement to turn his shipmates, who are grunting in the pigsty, back into human form, and she invites Odysseus to bring his remaining crew to the palace to feast and rest. Circe bathes and anoints them and clothes them with tunics and mantles. They feast at her abundant table. She upholds her oath not to harm them.

As Circe's guests, they remain on her island for a year. Finally, Odysseus' shipmates urge him to get back on track: "Captain, shake off this trance, and think of home— if home indeed awaits us." (X:472–474) Then Odysseus pleads with Circe to help him sail home. She agrees. She explains, however, that he must first visit the Underworld, the land of the dead, in order to hear the prophecy of the blind prophet Teiresias.

Odysseus and his men weep and despair when they hear this requirement, for they know there is no guarantee of return. Nevertheless, they have no choice if they are ever to reach home.

BALANCING THE INNER MASCULINE AND FEMININE

After enduring tremendous hardship and the loss of so many companions, Odysseus and his men no doubt ben-efit from their recharge on Circe's island. They stay a full year resting and easing their aching hearts, and Odysseus would willingly have stayed longer had not his shipmates urged him homeward.

There are different ways to look at this episode. From one perspective, we observe that if we do not focus we may get sidetracked and risk not reaching our goals. We cannot afford to stand still or we may get stuck. From another perspective, Odysseus and his men, hardened warriors all, linger with Circe while they develop their feminine side to balance their already strong masculine side.

Traditionally, as mentioned earlier, qualities that are more action- and goal-oriented, practical and analytical are said to be "masculine," while qualities that are intuitive, emotionally-sensitive, compassionate and nurturing are said to be "feminine." Again, both men and women need a healthy balance of all these aspects. As we have seen in earlier episodes, an unbalanced union of masculine and feminine forces brings weakness, not strength.

The episode with Circe is rich in symbolism. Tests related to wisdom, the archetypal quality of this trial, often deal with unity and connectedness, disunity and disconnectedness. In this trial Odysseus is tested on these as well as on his ability to maintain focus, to communicate clearly, and to reconcile opposites.

Early in the trial, the crew members come into contact with a feminine power that turns them into swine. They have given free rein to their greed and so they temporarily become what they have embodied, their piggish nature. Odysseus is saved from this fate by Hermes, the messenger of the gods. Hermes offers Odysseus an herb to keep his "mind and senses clear." It is the antidote to Circe's potion.

What do Hermes and his "good medicine" represent? The stoic philosopher Cleanthes said that *moly* "is an allegorical representation of the logos, by whose power the lower instincts and passions are made weaker."[4] I see Hermes and his *moly* as representing the inner teacher and grace. They also represent the higher mind, higher knowledge, or intuition that can help us pass our tests if we will listen and obey.

Tests of wisdom require us to keep a clear, focused mind. Odysseus does this. To subdue Circe, he uses a sharp sword, the symbol of discrimination, discernment and wisdom. Odysseus' mind is sharp; and he wields his intellect to good effect.

Odysseus uses his masterful skill in communication to get Circe to swear no further harm. With Hermes' good medicine and the sword, Odysseus is able to tame the feminine power, represented by Circe. When she invites him into her bed, she says "we two shall mingle." This invitation shows that he has mastered the energy that can unify opposites, male and female, and bring cohesion and wholeness.

But once Odysseus mingles his strong masculine energy with the feminine energy, he temporarily loses his balance, focus and sense of reality. He may be attempting to resolve the warring of opposing elements within himself, his mind and emotions, his lower desires and higher desires. He may be struggling to achieve a healthy inner balance of masculine and feminine qualities.

Maybe one part of Odysseus wants to stay with Circe, away from the challenges of the sea, and another part of him wants to undergo the trials that will bring him home. Since he cannot make up his mind, he goes no-where; he just stands still. Odysseus is subtly enchanted. By getting caught up with Circe, Odysseus, in effect, goes to sleep. The consequences are no less dire than they were when he fell asleep instead of guarding the bag of winds that Aiolos had given him. Thus, a year later, he is still with Circe and he is no closer to his goal. In fact, he has lost sight of his goal—union with his other half, his wife, Penelope, who is waiting for him to return.

In other words, Odysseus has lost his focused masculine force. Even though he must join forces with his feminine side to achieve balance, he also needs to retain his proactive, inner masculine protector that will see him all the way home. We saw earlier that the masculine with-out the balancing feminine becomes brutish. Now we see that the masculine overwhelmed by the feminine becomes weak.

Early in his journey homeward, in his trial in the land of the Lotus Eaters, Odysseus quickly overcame the temptation to escape into a blissful oblivion. But now, after so much heartbreak and loss, after having lost most of his men and eleven ships, his body worn, his heart torn, he may be finding it more challenging to summon the willpower he needs to keep going. Perhaps he finds it too painful to keep holding on to a desire that seems only to recede further into the distance. Eventually, though, his men urge him to remember his goal and to get back on course. He rallies.

Odysseus asserts his masculine drive by telling Circe that he must be on his way. Once he does, the femi-nine goddess works with him willingly. She offers helpful guidance for his journey, telling him the steps he has to take next. When the masculine and feminine forces are in balance, they work in tandem as two halves of the whole.

WISDOM AND DISCERNMENT

When Odysseus and his men first arrive at Circe's island, they are exhausted and in a deep state of grief. For all his drive and fortitude, Odysseus shows wisdom and discernment in the way he deals with his companions. He compassionately allows them to continue resting while he does the preliminary scouting. He rules out other possibilities before deciding that the only reasonable option is to look for someone who might help them. Since the disastrous encounters with the Cyclops and with the man-eating Laistrygones, however, he has learned not to charge rashly into the unknown.

After determining his course, Odysseus goes back to feed his men and take care of their needs before sending out a scouting party. When the stag crosses his path, Odysseus sees it as divine providence and brings it back for their feast. He heartens them with kind words of encouragement and then allows one more day of rest before announcing his plan. Showing both discernment and sensitivity, he gives a rallying talk and then, rather than appointing men as scouts, they draw lots to determine who will explore the island.

In tune with his inner wisdom, Odysseus receives the messenger of the gods, Hermes, and follows a careful plan to avoid Circe's trap. Later on, however, he gets distracted until the men remind him of his goal of returning home. One way to see this incident is that without a sustained focus, even someone with a shrewd intellect and good intuition can be challenged in staying true to a plan and following through.

We all have access to inner wisdom. When we tune in to that wisdom, we can better understand what we are to do next and the steps we need to take to make it happen.

First we have to conceive of a plan. Before we bring it into the physical, we have to assess whether it is practical. If it is, then we can summon our forces to make it a reality. We might need to consult experts or enlist others to help us. In short, we do everything we can to make that project work.

If we have a burning desire to do and be something, we find it easy to pour our energy and creativity into it. Analyzing our passion(s) and then forming a clear vision of our mission will help us to identify our top priorities and then train our focus on them. We may have many interests, many desires, but to accomplish any of them we will likely need to focus on our top one or two, and then put all of our energy, creativity, training and service into achieving them. This is what Odysseus' men did for him. When he got stuck, they reminded him of his highest goal and helped to get him back on track.

Five o'Clock Line

TESTS OF WISDOM

STRENGTHS	WEAKNESSES
wise dominion; tethered to higher self	envy, jealousy; ignores higher self
quick-thinking and acting; learns quickly; intuitive	impatient, not thorough, high-strung, fragmented
versatile, adaptable	dual personality; changeable, wavering
thirsty for knowledge, mentally "alive"	unfocused, discontented; needs constant mental stimulation
ability to see all sides of a question; perceptive	can appear fickle, self-contradictory
articulate, eloquent; freely shares knowledge	talks too much; unable to slow down and listen

WHO AM I?
FIVE O'CLOCK LINE: WISDOM

Take a moment to think about wisdom in your life. Reflect on the chart of strengths and weaknesses and use it to evaluate your expressions of wisdom. Later in this chapter, you will have an opportunity to map your strategy for turning weaknesses into strengths.

What are my greatest strengths in relation to wisdom?

_____
_____
_____

What are my greatest weaknesses in relation to wisdom?

_____
_____
_____

Thus far in my life, how have I handled challenges involving aspects of wisdom? Would I handle any of those situations differently now? How?

_____
_____
_____

What can I learn about myself and wisdom from Odysseus' experience? Is there anyone who was a Circe in my life at some point?

_____
_____
_____

WINNING STRATEGIES
FIVE O'CLOCK LINE: WISDOM

KEEP YOUR MIND AND SENSES CLEAR. Hermes gave Odysseus the *moly* plant to keep his mind and senses clear. What is it that keeps you focused? What do you do to keep yourself from running off in all directions at once? Your focusing tool may be a period of solitude or exercise, music or art, or contacting the earth by spending time in nature.

Participate regularly in whatever helps to keep you in touch with your higher self and focused.

STAY FOCUSED AND ALERT. It takes a strong mind to stay mentally alert, to resist the temptation to succumb to the subtle pulls that make you forget where you are really going. If you let down your guard, you may find yourself at the mercy of your own lesser desires, other people's requests or lesser desires, or other distractions that are detours from pursuing your soul's destiny. For instance, even if you need regeneration from a debilitating illness or other experience, be sensitive about when you can move on in your mission.

Watch out for enticing or just overly comfortable situations that distract you from your focus.

DEFINE YOUR TOP PRIORITIES IN LIFE. To know what is most important in our life, we have to know clearly what our goals are. If you don't have a mission in life, you may have a tendency to meander. Look at projects you started but never finished. Will you ever get back to them? Are they really related to achieving your major life goals? If you are a jack-of-all-trades, you may need to choose among the things you do well and enjoy. If this sounds limiting, consider the alternative:

If you don't determine what to focus on, your energy may be too scattered, hindering the thrust needed to accomplish your mission or an important goal.

DEVELOP A PRACTICAL ACTION PLAN FOR WHAT YOU WANT TO ACCOMPLISH. Some practical steps you might take are to make to-do lists and set a timeline. This takes analytical abilities. You can also take time for reflection to allow inspiration and innovation to percolate into your conscious awareness. It often takes both analysis and inspiration to sort out, schedule and make real progress on a project.

Determining an action plan and following through to completion even on small projects will help you to create a momentum that will carry you through on your major goals.

BALANCE YOUR MASCULINE AND FEMININE QUALITIES. To varying degrees, most of us need to work on balancing our inner masculine and feminine natures. Although there may be situations that call for more of one or the other, when you have a balanced approach you can be intuitive and receive inspiration from your higher self but also be down-to-earth, analyzing alternatives and choosing practical actions to take. Sometimes hobbies or avocations can provide the balance to the work or activity we normally do.

If you work on achieving the masculine and feminine balance of your inner being, the success of all your endeavors will be enhanced.

WHERE AM I GOING?
FIVE O'CLOCK LINE: WISDOM

As you reflect on the following questions, you may find it helpful to review the various aspects of wisdom in the chart on p. 131 and "The Stuff Heroes Are Made Of" on pp. 4–5, as well as the Winning Strategies. Using the questions below, map out a strategy to apply the insights you've gained.

In the tests of wisdom presented by my current life circumstances, how can I use my strengths constructively?

_____

_____

How can I turn any weakness I may have into an expression of wisdom that I can claim as a new strength?

_____

_____

If I have a tendency to more masculine qualities, being action-oriented, practical and analytical, or feminine qualities, such as inspiration, intuition and sensitivity, what are some things I can do to find a balance that supports my inner wholeness?

_____

_____

What can I use as my moly herb that will help me to have clarity about important decisions? What will enhance the sword of my mind to discern the best actions to take?

_____

_____

THE MEETING OF TWO PERSONALITIES
IS LIKE THE CONTACT OF TWO CHEMICAL
SUBSTANCES: IF THERE IS ANY REACTION,
BOTH ARE TRANSFORMED.

C. G. JUNG

Six o'Clock Line

JOURNEY TO THE UNDERWORLD

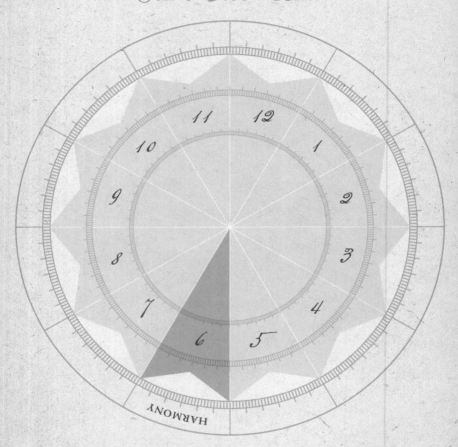

Six o'Clock Line

JOURNEY TO THE UNDERWORLD

But you must long for the daylight. Go, quickly.
ODYSSEUS' MOTHER

When Odysseus hears that he must travel to the Underworld, he asks: "Circe, who will be our guide on that journey? No one has ever yet in a black ship gone all the way to Hades." The goddess replies, "Only set up your mast pole and spread the white sails upon it, and sit still, and let the blast of the North Wind carry you." (X:501–502, 505–507)

Before sending off Odysseus and his men, the goddess offers him precise instruction for the treacherous undertaking. She outlines rituals he must follow and promises he must make many times "to the strengthless heads of the perished dead" if he is to succeed. "Then," she says, "the prophet will soon come to you, and he will tell you the way to go, the stages of your journey, and tell you how to make your way home." (X:521–522, 538–540)

Odysseus follows Circe's instruction to the letter. Soon the famed blind prophet Teiresias, who foretells his future trials, draws near and partakes of Odysseus' offering. Then Teiresias prophesies. He says that Odysseus desires only "a sweet, smooth journey home" but that Poseidon will make his journey hard because Odysseus blinded the god's dear son Polyphemus, the Cyclops. "Even so," says Teiresias, "you and your crew may still reach home,

The blind prophet Teiresias prophesies, "Even so, you and your crew may still reach home, suffering all the way."

suffering all the way, if you only have the power to curb their wild desire and curb your own." (XI:100, 104–105)

In particular, the prophet warns Odysseus that when the crew stops at the land of Helios, the sun god, they must not harm his cattle. If they do, he says, the ship and the men will all be destroyed. Even if Odysseus survives such a catastrophe, he will reach home a broken man. His house will be filled with crude, arrogant men who are eating his livestock and courting his wife.

Odysseus speaks next with the ghost of his dead mother. She tells him that she did not die from a natural illness but from grief. She says, "Only my loneliness for you, Odysseus, for your kind heart and counsel, gentle Odysseus, took my own life away." Three times he tries to embrace her and comfort her, but she slips through his fingers like a shadow, dissolving "like a dream." (XI:202–203, 207–208)

Then Odysseus converses with the ghosts of "a grand array of women," wives and daughters of illustrious men. (XI:225–226) Each one, in turn, tells her story of fortune or of woe. He also meets the ghost of Agamemnon, supreme commander of the campaign against Troy. Agamemnon is brooding over his past. He tells Odysseus that upon his return from the Trojan War, his unfaithful wife and her lover murdered him. He warns Odysseus: "Indulge a woman never." (XI:441)

After this, Odysseus sees the ghost of Achilles, the great hero of the Trojan War. Odysseus complains to him: "My life is endless trouble. But you, Achilles, there's not a man in the world more blest than you." He encourages Achilles not to grieve since he now reigns over all the dead. In return, Achilles chides him: "No winning words about death to *me*, shining Odysseus! By god, I'd rather slave on earth for another man—some dirt-poor tenant farmer who scrapes to keep alive—than rule down here over all the breathless dead." (XI:482–483, 488–491)

Odysseus meets many other ghosts of the dead. Finally hordes of them gather around to talk to him, and he rushes off in terror.

EXPLORING THE DEPTHS

In this trial, Odysseus delves into the Underworld. In the world's mythology and spiritual traditions, many heroes have undertaken this journey, among them Jesus, Gilgamesh and Dante. In symbolic terms, the journey to the Underworld is an exploration of our own depths, our unconscious.

Why does this journey seem to be a rite of passage for heroes? For one thing, there is wisdom in our unconscious that we cannot access elsewhere. Like Odysseus, each of us is a hero in the making. We cannot get beyond a certain point in our personal odyssey until we deal with the contents of the unconscious, bring forth its hidden wisdom, and use it to attain higher levels of being.

Based on what is in our unconscious, a positive prophecy and a negative prophecy awaits each of us. If we do not recognize and deal with our unconscious in a timely way, we will eventually play out the negative prophecy. What do we have in our own underworld—a Cyclops or a Circe? If we will unearth and transform the patterns and forms that are buried in our unconscious, we will see the positive prophecy come to pass.

The message of the prophet Teiresias to Odysseus reflects the true nature of prophecy. Prophecy is not a prediction set in stone, but a warning of what may happen if there is not a change in behavior.

THE SHADOW

Carl Jung said, "One does not become enlightened by imagining figures of light, but by making darkness conscious."[5] Jung was talking about dealing with our "shadow," the unconscious aspects of ourselves that we are not aware of or that we repress. This is what Odysseus does during his entire journey. He comes face to face with the shadowed, or hidden, parts of himself that take the form of giants, monsters, temptresses, lotus-eaters—the shapes of his own ego, greed and fear.

In her book *Riding the Dragon*, author Roselle Angwin notes the importance of dealing with the shadow:

> *In contrast to the ego, the Shadow is unconscious, and contains and embodies those aspects of ourselves that we don't know or we don't like.... Marie-Louise von Franz, [a disciple of Jung],...calls the Shadow "the dark, unlit and repressed sides of the ego-complex."...*
>
> *By definition,...it is difficult for us to see our own Shadow, despite the fact that it follows close behind us wherever we go, and is perfectly clear to anyone else!...*
>
> *We know when someone else has stepped on our Shadow by our over-reaction to them; the Shadow is projected "out there," so that what we hate or fear most in another person, what makes us uncomfortable or angry, is a clue to what needs to be acknowledged and*

made conscious in our lives. The only way most of us
can start to recognize and own the Shadow is by paying
careful attention to our own negative feelings....

By paying careful attention to our negative feelings in response to others, we can begin to recognize and
own our shadow. What we see in another that makes us
angry or hurt or uneasy or threatened or envious indicates
a point of nonresolution within ourselves. It is almost as if
we are riding around in bumper cars and we keep bump-
ing into the same people or the same situation. Until we
bring our shadow to light, we keep going round and round
and round.

Angwin continues:

The Shadow is not always negative—it also contains
our own unlived positive qualities, too, and much of our
joy and creativity. Whoever is willing to turn and face
their Shadow releases an enormous potential energy, an
abundance of joy and spontaneity....

To meet and embrace the Shadow brings new
life.... The more violently we repress the negative aspects
of ourselves, the more likely we are to project this nega-
tivity onto the outer world at large, onto our friends,
neighbors, lovers, parents, society, or even whole races.[6]

WHOLENESS REQUIRES INNER HARMONY

In this trial, Odysseus is dealing with desires, emotions
and the unconscious as well as his psychological roots and
family influences, especially his mother. In his visit to the
Underworld, Odysseus encounters his mother and many

other women. The message to him is that he must develop the compassionate, motherly side of his nature. He is given a chance to do this as he hears the story of each of the ghosts.

More importantly, Odysseus receives a message from his mother, who, representing his feminine side, tells him that she died because she missed his "kind heart" and gentleness. The message his unconscious is conveying to him is: "Develop your kind heart and your gentleness, for without them you cannot be whole and you will ultimately perish."

On the other hand, Odysseus is warned by Agamemnon to "indulge a woman never." In psychological terms, this warning reads: "Never indulge the *unredeemed* feminine." This advice applies equally to men and women. It means never to indulge the *distorted* feminine nature's untempered emotions, moodiness, melancholy and over-sensitivity.

In Odysseus' earlier trials we saw that his strong masculine side without the complementary feminine side becomes brutish and, conversely, that the masculine overwhelmed by the feminine becomes weak. Now we see that when the feminine is not balanced by the masculine, inner harmony is compromised. Correspondingly, the prophet Teiresias warns Odysseus that he must deal with his desire body—he must tame his "wild desires" or he will not make it home. The underlying message is that wholeness requires inner harmony, and to achieve this requires a balance between the masculine and feminine sides of our being. The requirement for change is clear: If Odysseus and his crew can hold at bay the passions that caused them to fail or do poorly in previous tests, they will all make it home. If they do not, their unredeemed actions will bring disaster upon them.

Teiresias highlights one of the major lessons Odysseus has to learn: Do not indulge in excesses or extremes but be self-controlled and take the middle way—not too far to one side or the other. As we have seen, Odysseus has a habit of being excessive. He excessively kills and loots at Troy and Ismaros. He parades his ego before the Cyclops instead of holding his tongue. He guards the bag of winds by himself instead of sharing the responsibility.

We have also seen Odysseus succumb to the opposite extreme, passivity. He falls asleep while guarding the bag of winds just when he is coming within sight of his homeland. He languishes with Circe for a year.

In his remaining trials, Odysseus will undergo tests of harmony and balance, tests of taking the middle way, again and again: Will he fight when he is told not to? Will he passively give in to his men when they badger him? Will he once again surrender to a seductress? Will he maintain self-control when he finally reaches Ithaca and encounters the suitors who have invaded his household? We will see.

A PASSION FOR LIFE

One of the traits of a hero is a willingness to let go of the past. Revolving what is behind us leaves us vulnerable to the pitfalls of moodiness and melancholy. Each of the ghosts who speak to Odysseus is reviewing his or her past. Each has a tale that unveils the consequences of actions taken. Listening to their tales gives Odysseus an opportunity to learn valuable lessons. For example, some of the ghosts, like the brooding Agamemnon, see themselves as victims. Odysseus' response is to keep his own inner balance and harmony; he does not yield to the temptation to drown in past sorrows.

Odysseus is learning not to engage in self-pity and see himself as a victim. He is tempted to do so. Imagine how he must feel: Many of his men have been killed or eaten by giants or monsters. All but one of the ships he started with have been destroyed along with their crews. He came within sight of his homeland only to be blown far, far away. On several occasions he and his remaining crew have barely escaped disaster. And now Teiresias prophesies that before Odysseus regains his home he will suffer many more hardships.

In the face of all that, anyone might be tempted to think that death is enticing. And yet, when Odysseus complains to Achilles that his life is endless trouble, Achilles sets him straight. He tells Odysseus that life is more precious by far than death could ever be.

At the end of his journey to the Underworld, Odysseus passes a major test of harmony: He rejects self-pity and passivity in favor of valor. He looks death squarely in the face and decides to return to the land of the living.

Choosing life is not limited to physical life and death, for death is not something that happens only when the heart stops beating. Death occurs when we no longer have the spiritual fire to ignite our soul and keep that flame burning strong. To give up on life is to commit spiritual suicide. Spiritual suicide is subtle; it refers to those who give up while they are still physically alive. By maintaining a strong passion for life and for our mission and destiny, we keep that fire burning.

MAKING DARKNESS LIGHT

To become whole requires that we brave the painful and sometimes shocking trials of wrestling with our own self-made monsters. By doing so, we liberate the energy that is trapped in them. Various psychological and spiritual tools can help us with our inner work of self-liberation. But beware: The hammer approach will not work. This is not a process of smashing an unwanted or unappealing part of ourselves; it is a process of transmutation. To *transmute* something is to change it into a higher form.

By acknowledging the archetypes within ourselves, we can transform the negatives into positives. For instance, we can transform tyranny into willpower; ambition and pride into self-assertiveness; duality into integration; self-pity into emotional sensitivity.

Shadow qualities can also be positive and in our inner journey we can also claim those. However, we are unlikely to express them in a positive way until we become consciously aware of them. Most of us are more aware of the negative shadow qualities than we are of the positive. Even reading these words might trigger thoughts about some negative aspect or character trait. If some negative trait just popped into your mind, ask yourself, *What is the ideal quality that is the positive counterpart of* [negative trait]? This little exercise can offer you a glimpse of your shadow side.

If we will reflect on the ideal quality of any shadow aspect that we do not like within ourselves and then begin to cultivate that ideal quality, we will begin transforming that shadow aspect into its pristine, positive expression. On the surface we may be expressing a negative aspect, and yet at the unconscious level lies dormant the seed of the divine potential of which the surface behavior, attitude, emotion, or action is just the other side of the coin.

One way to access and cultivate our positive qualities is to consciously notice the things we deeply enjoy in life. When we notice positive qualities in others that really touch our heart, we can claim those qualities for ourselves. The reason we recognize them in others is because they are already within us. In this way we can start recognizing our own inner beauty, the beauty of our soul that we might otherwise not perceive.

Accessing these archetypal positives takes work. Finding the gold in our unconscious can be likened to the process of mining gold from ore that is embedded in rock and soil. We may have to go deep into our unconscious to find the golden qualities that are there and that will express who we really are.

INNER WISDOM

Some people find it difficult to make important decisions. Those who do may always have had someone telling them what to do, and so they have been conditioned to following orders and directives from others. While that approach may seem to work well in the short term, it is essential that we move beyond that stage. When a decision is ours to make, the voice to heed is the voice of the higher self. It is so important that we reach the place where we know from within what we should do and also have the conviction to follow our inner guidance.

If we make mistakes, that is okay. One key to effective decision making is another of the traits of a hero, the willingness to make mistakes and to learn from them. The more decisions we make, the more effective we will be at interpreting and following our inner guidance. The result will be that we make better and better decisions.

If decision making is new territory for you, start by making small decisions. That way, if things do not turn out as you had hoped, you will find it easier to get up and try again the next time. It is also important not to let that "next time" be so far down the road that you lose the courage to build this skill. With practice, all of us can reach the place where, like Odysseus, we feel confident making the important decisions that will take us home to our higher self and lead to our victory in life.

☮ ANCHORING YOUR INSIGHTS ☮

Six o'Clock Line

TESTS OF HARMONY

STRENGTHS	WEAKNESSES
developed inner feminine; nurturing; serves others	martyr complex; gives up on life; lacks fire and courage
powerful imagination	stuck in the past, caught up in things that do not exist
in harmony with personal odyssey	indecisive, self-justifying, confused
emotionally sensitive	overly sensitive, self-pitying, moody
loving, caring, protective in relationships	possessive, relationship-dependent
intuitive; protective empathy	withdrawing, distant, timid

WHO AM I?

SIX O'CLOCK LINE: HARMONY

Take a moment to think about harmony in your life. Reflect on the chart of strengths and weaknesses and use it to evaluate your expressions of harmony. Later in this chapter, you will have an opportunity to map your strategy for turning weaknesses into strengths.

What are my greatest strengths in relation to harmony?

_____

_____

_____

What are my greatest weaknesses in relation to harmony? What strengths would be their positive counterparts?

_____

_____

_____

Thus far in my life, how have I handled challenges involving aspects of harmony? Would I handle any of those situations differently now? How?

_____

_____

_____

What can I learn about myself and harmony from Odysseus' experience?

_____

_____

_____

Winning Strategies

SIX O'CLOCK LINE: HARMONY

KEEP ON KEEPING ON. We all start new ventures with enthusiasm and a sense of empowerment. These traits will carry us a certain distance, but we may go through extreme difficulty from within or without before reaching the goal line. If strong emotions well up from the unconscious, you may feel drained, discouraged, depressed or angry. Or someone may become angry or upset with you and knock the wind out of your sails. You may be downhearted and feel like your life is filled with troubles, as Odysseus complained to Achilles. If you feel like giving up, pull yourself together and continue to take one step forward at a time. Even if the steps you take are baby steps, you can keep moving forward with whatever you undertake. We do not have to conquer the world all at once.

As long as you keep moving forward, you will eventually reach the light at the end of the tunnel. Keep your eye on the light!

TRANSCEND THE PAST BY RESOLVING IT. Learn the lessons that your past and your unconscious have to offer, but don't get stuck there. As George Santayana said, "Those who cannot remember the past are condemned to repeat it." But wallowing in guilt or self-pity or continuing to see yourself as a victim can be a huge stumbling block on your odyssey. Victims cannot be healed. As long as a wound remains open, it cannot heal. Until you resolve whatever issue lies at the core of your psychological wounds, those wounds won't heal and you won't move on. When we have this kind of wound, it's not really about the other person; it's about us. And we can decide who we are and how we deal with experiences in life. Once you internalize the lessons of the past, those lessons will become a part of your inner wisdom.

Resolve your past, and you will move forward and continue to grow.

CURB INORDINATE DESIRES AND PASSIONS. If we entertain many different desires or have conflicting desires, it may be difficult for us to anticipate what a fulfilled future would look like, and even more difficult to get there. Refer to the strengths listed in the chart for each of the twelve archetypal qualities to get a clear picture of what it means to pour your passion into something positive.

Being in harmony with your higher self in the balance of power, wisdom and love will give you everything you need to fulfill your heart's true desires.

WATCH OUT FOR THE UNREDEEMED FEMININE IN YOUR EMOTIONS. The feminine side of a man or woman is the feeling side—caring, nurturing, intuitive, sensitive to beauty and in tune with the inner self. When the feminine is repressed, then tenderness, affection and receptivity are also repressed. Men or women with unbalanced feminine energy may fall into a wide range of untempered emotions: cold and distant, sulky, moody, oversensitive, passive, self-pitying, withdrawn, sarcastic or angry.

When your feminine side fully supports your masculine side, your soul is more beautifully and fully expressed in your achievements in life.

WHERE AM I GOING?
SIX O'CLOCK LINE: HARMONY

As you reflect on the following questions, you may find it helpful to review the various aspects of harmony in the chart on p. 153 and "The Stuff Heroes Are Made Of" on pp. 4–5, as well as the Winning Strategies. Using the questions below, map out a strategy to apply the insights you've gained.

In the tests of harmony presented by my current life circumstances, how can I use my strengths constructively?

_____

_____

_____

How can I turn any shadow aspect I have identified in myself into an archetypal expression of harmony that I can claim as a new strength?

_____

_____

_____

Where might I express more of my feminine side in positive ways?

_____

_____

_____

How can I engage my passion for life to overcome any discouragement I may be experiencing in my endeavors?

_____

_____

_____

ONE DAY YOUR LIFE WILL
FLASH BEFORE YOUR EYES. MAKE SURE
IT'S WORTH WATCHING.

UNKNOWN SOURCE

BULGARIA

START

Istanbul

Kazan

Komotini

Maronia

Canakkale

Troy

GREECE

END

TUR

Athens

Mycenae

Pylos

Sparta

CRETE

FOLLOWING

Seven o'Clock Line

THE LURE OF GLORY

Seven o'Clock Line

GRATITUDE

THE LURE OF GLORY

*We must steer clear of the Sirens, their
enchanting song, their meadow starred with flowers.
I alone was to hear their voices...but you must
bind me with tight, chafing ropes.*

ODYSSEUS

After leaving the Underworld, Odysseus and his men
return briefly to Circe's island. She tells Odysseus how he
can survive his next trials. She explains that his journey
will soon take him near the island of the Sirens, "creatures
who spellbind any man alive, whoever comes their way." In
a pile beside the Sirens are the bones of dead men rotting
away. Circe warns Odysseus: "Whoever draws too close,
off guard, and catches the Sirens' voices in the air" (XII:39–
42) will never reach home, for he becomes transfixed by
their irresistible song.

Circe advises Odysseus to race straight past the
Siren's coast. She tells him to plug his oarsmen's ears with
beeswax so that none of the crew can hear the Sirens'
song. The goddess says, however, that if Odysseus wants
to listen to the Sirens, he must first have his men lash him

hand and foot to the mast. And when he cries out to be untied, they should only twist more rope around him.

Odysseus shares with his crew Circe's warning for making it safely by the alluring voices of the Sirens. Determined to hear their enchanting song himself, he tells his men, "Only I, she said, was to listen to them." He repeats Circe's precise instructions for securing him to the mast with "rope on pressing rope." (XII:159–160, 164) As he passes by, lashed to the mast, he hears them singing to him:

> *Come closer, famous Odysseus—Achaea's pride and glory—moor your ship on our coast so you can hear our song! Never has any sailor passed our shores in his black craft until he has heard the honeyed voices pouring from our lips, and once he hears to his heart's content sails on, a wiser man. We know all the pains that Achaeans and Trojans once endured on the spreading plain of Troy when the gods willed it so—all that comes to pass on the fertile earth, we know it all! (XII:184–191)*

SWEET MUSIC TO THE EGO

In this episode, Odysseus' trial comes in the guise of music, the "high, thrilling song" of the Sirens. To hear their "ravishing voices" makes his heart throb to listen longer. On one level, the Sirens represent flattery that appeals to Odysseus' desire for recognition and praise. Circe said that Odysseus could "have joy in hearing the song of the Sirens." (XII:181–183; XII:52) Yet he must secure himself "with rope on pressing rope" against the lure of glory. Flattery, however sweet its music is to the ego, it is not a solution that fulfills our need for love. Rather than

Odysseus says, "I tried to say 'Untie me!' to the crew,…but they bent steady to the oars."

needing flattery, which is insincere or excessive praise, all of us, adults and children alike, need positive recognition and praise that is merited.

On another level, the Sirens' song represents the lure of so-called higher knowledge at the expense of our earthly duties. The Sirens claim to know all that comes to pass on earth, and they tempt Odysseus with knowledge that no ordinary mortal has. He must hold fast against the lure of glory in this aspect also.

The offer of such knowledge is a formidable temptation—the promise of being elevated above all mortals, of knowing all things. In truth, the knowledge of all things will not help us, because our higher self already knows and imparts to us, as we require it, all the knowledge we need to fulfill our destiny. Until we have need of it, knowledge will not serve us well but may serve to distract us, leaving us to idle away our life. The pursuit of knowledge for the sake of knowledge may cause us to ignore our obligations to the people who need us the most.

Odysseus knows that he is needed at home, and reaching home is his cherished goal. Had he stopped to tarry with the Sirens, he would never have reached home and the knowledge he gained would have served no purpose. His whitened bones would eventually have laid scattered on the shore along with those of many others who succumbed to their thrilling promise.

More than anything else, Odysseus desires to see his wife and son and to reclaim his place in his kingdom. Thus, although he chooses to hear the Sirens' song for the enjoyment it promises to bring him, he follows Circe's explicit instructions to have himself tied securely to the mast. He gives clear commands to his men not to undo the ropes, no matter how much he might command them or plead, until they are safely past the danger. If Odysseus had allowed flattery to catch him off guard, he would not have been able to resist its allure.

Another theme in the episode with the Sirens is effective leadership. Odysseus is tested on his ability as a leader to raise up others. He successfully passes this test by plugging the ears of his crew members to protect them from temptation. They, in turn, resist any temptation to remove the wax from their ears.

If Odysseus had not been strong on this line, he

could have been blinded by his own ambition and acted without regard for his crew. He could have lost emotional control or refused to be secured to the mast. Instead, he displays courage and warm-hearted leadership. He is thoughtful and sensitive to the needs of his companions. As a result, his men follow his lead. In short, he and his crew work harmoniously to get safely past the Sirens.

BLIND SPOTS

In order to master any quality, we have to know what that quality looks and feels like when we are exhibiting it in either its positive or negative aspects. This takes an awareness of how it feels to us internally, in our bodies. To learn how our behavior looks and feels to others, we can ask a trusted friend for feedback. Achieving awareness is more than a mental exercise. It may take a concerted effort of all of our faculties to recognize these traits when we are in the midst of them. For example, we might consider the ways in which we have demonstrated gratitude to others as well as times when we have been ungrateful, thoughtless or inconsiderate. Were we conscious of our attitude and behavior at the time, or are we seeing it only in retrospect?

More often than not, behaving with ingratitude, thoughtlessness or inconsideration is something we do unconsciously. When we are in the midst of expressing a negative trait or pattern, we are in a vortex in which we will not necessarily see, know or understand. Others who see us *will* see, know and understand the trait or pattern we are caught up in, but we will not, because we are at a point of spiritual blindness. It is also easier for us to notice when others exhibit certain behaviors than it is to identify them in ourselves.

In a state of spiritual blindness, we confuse our lesser self with our higher self. We identify with our ego, and in this state we are not able to enter or probe the realms of higher consciousness. Yet if we do not know what our blind spot is, what it really looks or feels like when we are exhibiting it, then how can we ever overcome it? If we do not receive positive attention and genuine praise from ourselves, we will look to others to fill our need, whether in a positive way or by drawing negative attention to ourselves.

When we engage in negative patterns and behaviors, it is because we do not see ourselves clearly. We cannot effectively change things that we cannot see and do not understand. To be able to make changes, we have to become conscious of ourselves and our behavior. It is often easy to be aware of certain patterns when we see them in others. But we may not always be conscious of ourselves or notice our own flaws. There can be a fine line between the positive and negative expressions of a quality.

Consider, for example, ambition. A healthy ambition drives people to fulfill their studies and training, to excel, to achieve great things, to fulfill their reason for being. When ambition is in balance and is tempered by other qualities, it is a positive quality. But when ambition is untempered by concern for others, it is negative. In its negative aspect, ambition can make us blind to the needs of others. When we are in a vortex of blind ambition, we may ruthlessly pursue what we want even if it violates the needs and freedom of others. Odysseus demonstrated this in the Cyclops' cave and in the attack on Ismaros.

TETHERED TO THE MAST OF REALITY

Circe explains to Odysseus that in order to survive the trial presented by the Sirens and make progress on his homeward journey, he must not only tie himself to the mast but must also take care of his men. He follows through, and by ensuring that those around him have what they need to get safely past the beguiling voices of the Sirens, he ensures the safe passage of all.

If we consider that the crew members represent aspects of Odysseus' character, then we could say that Odysseus is being tested on the limits of his self-control. The way he handles this test demonstrates that he is learning a lesson he handled poorly in the Cyclops episode. In this current trial with the Sirens, Odysseus effectively straightjackets his ego and makes himself (his crew) deaf to flattery and the lure of glory and knowledge. With his lesser self securely under control, he survives the temptation and does not allow himself to be moved or distracted from his goal.

Odysseus is needed at home and his strongest desire is to reach home. To reach this goal, part of his focus has to be on meeting the needs of his crew. He could not have successfully completed this stage of his voyage without also attending to those who were around him.

This lesson applies to all of us on our odyssey to wholeness. As we strive to reach our goals we must not neglect the people who are around us, for the real work of the spirit takes place in the streets of life. If we are not tied to the mast of reality, we may ignore the work that must take place in the physical world. Mother Teresa demonstrated this principle in her tremendous service to the people of Calcutta. In her centers and in the streets, with love and respect, she served the physical needs of those who so desperately needed care—those whose bodies needed bathing, whose bellies needed feeding, or who were literally taking their last breaths.

We are needed by people who cannot get by without our assistance, whether they are family, friends, coworkers, neighbors, or strangers we meet along the way. Can we open our heart to tutor a child? To mentor a teen? To care for and comfort the elderly and ill? To ease the struggle of a parent who must juggle work and the care of a family? As we reach out to help others, our heart opens in gratitude for the many blessings in our own life, and we are further blessed.

To make progress on our soul's odyssey requires practical application. Carl Jung faced this test when immersed in his work. In his book *Memories, Dreams, Reflections*, Jung says: "It was most essential for me to have a normal life in the real world as a counterpoise to that strange inner world [of work with fantasies].... The unconscious contents could have driven me out of my wits. But my family, and the knowledge [that] I have a medical diploma from a Swiss university, I must help my patients, I have a wife and five children, I live at 228 Seestrasse in Küsnacht—these were actualities which made demands upon me and proved to me again and again that I really existed....

"No matter how deeply absorbed or how blown about I was, I always knew that everything I was experiencing was ultimately directed at this real life of mine. I meant to meet its obligations and fulfill its meanings."[7]

Jung wrote that his attention to the demands of the physical world kept him from "whirling about in the winds of the spirit."[8] His strong sense of obligation to his patients and his ties to his family and home tethered him to the mast of reality. Meeting the demands of physical reality functioned to hold open the door for him not only to probe the depths of the psyche but also to return from that realm to share his profound insights with the world.

⊕ ANCHORING YOUR INSIGHTS ⊕

Seven o'Clock Line

TESTS OF GRATITUDE

STRENGTHS	WEAKNESSES
able to discipline ego and work with others	ingratitude, thoughtlessness, spiritual blindness
strong leadership ability	proud, domineering, impetuous
has integrity which justifies having authority as a leader	thoughtless, lazy, inconstant
shows gratitude by using abilities to help others	uses abilities and gifts to glorify self
warm-hearted, magnanimous, expressive	excessive need for praise; center of attention
optimistic, cheerful	devastated when depressed

WHO AM I?
SEVEN O'CLOCK LINE: GRATITUDE

Take a moment to think about gratitude in your life. Reflect on the chart of strengths and weaknesses and use it to evaluate your expressions of gratitude. Later in this chapter, you will have an opportunity to map your strategy for turning weaknesses into strengths.

What are my greatest strengths in relation to gratitude?

_____

_____

_____

What are my greatest weaknesses in relation to gratitude, especially involving blind spots in my self-awareness?

_____

_____

_____

Thus far in my life, how have I handled challenges involving aspects of gratitude or spiritual blindness? Would I handle any of those situations differently now? How?

_____

_____

_____

What can I learn about myself and gratitude from Odysseus' experience?

_____

_____

_____

WINNING STRATEGIES
SEVEN O'CLOCK LINE: GRATITUDE

CULTIVATE HUMILITY AND GRATITUDE. No one has ever reached a goal without having received help, nurturing, support, or guidance somewhere along life's way. Learn to distinguish the subtle voice of flattery. Giving in to the alluring voices of the Sirens can take you far from your goals. True worth comes from within, from your connection to your higher self.

When you are tempted to take sole credit for your accomplishments and to bask in flattery, remember to feel gratitude for all who have helped you get to where you are today.

STAY TETHERED TO THE MAST OF REALITY. Your mast is whatever serves to keep you tethered to reality and focused on your goals when temptations come your way. To resist the call of the Sirens, Odysseus had himself tied to the mast of his ship, his means of reaching home. Jung's mast (his family and professional obligations) allowed him to keep a grip on reality while exploring the depths of the psyche.

Discover what it is that will keep you on track. When you are securely tied to your mast, you can do all of your inner work and also get out in the streets of life and interact with your fellowman. Obsessive self-analysis leads nowhere.

What will keep you focused on being love in action?

GET GUIDANCE AND HELP FROM OTHERS. During a test, it is easy to be tempted to center on yourself. But centering on yourself can create blindness or confusion about what is really going on. For example, "Is so-

and-so really trying to damage my reputation, or am I just reacting because my ego is wounded?"

Gentle and honest feedback from trusted friends can help you put things in perspective. Your friends are like Odysseus' crew, who tied more ropes around him when he tried to free himself from the mast. Good friends can hold you back when they see you trying to wriggle away from reality or heading into danger. If you share with them the negative traits you desire to overcome, they can support you and also warn you if they see you getting off track.

Ask your friends to keep you tied securely to your mast.

BE A SERVANT LEADER. SHARE CENTER STAGE WITH OTHERS. We all have a need to be loved and appreciated. But can we also support the talents and potential of other people? A true measure of success is whether or not we have used our talents to bring out the best in others. Odysseus carefully instructs and protects his companions from temptation. By doing so he gives them an opportunity to save the day. And they come through for him.

When you are tempted to take center stage, you might pause and consider whether this is a good opportunity to strengthen someone else who can, with encouragement, gain the confidence to push forward. If you do this from time to time, you will soon see it as another way to earn the love and appreciation that you long for.

A great leader raises up others.

FORGET YOURSELF IN THE GIVING OF SELF. The more gratitude and love you feel and express for the experiences of your life, the more you will feel gratitude and love returning to you and expanding within you. When gratitude so fills your heart that it spills over, you cannot help but share what you have received with others.

In fact, gratitude for gifts and abilities is best expressed by putting them into action for others. When you feel and express gratitude consistently, your whole life begins to go better. Giving to others is a sure antidote to pride and self-absorption, because in giving of yourself you literally forget about yourself.

Pride cannot grow in a garden full of love.

WHERE AM I GOING?
SEVEN O'CLOCK LINE: GRATITUDE

As you reflect on the following questions, you may find it helpful to review the various aspects of gratitude in the chart on p. 172 and "The Stuff Heroes Are Made Of" on pp. 4–5, as well as the Winning Strategies. Using the questions below, map out a strategy to apply the insights you've gained.

In the tests of gratitude presented by my current life circumstances, how can I use my strengths constructively?

_____
_____
_____

How can I turn any weakness I may have into an expression of gratitude that I can claim as a new strength?

_____
_____

What is my mast of reality that will keep me tied to my service to life? Which of my friends, family or associates can help keep me tied to my mast?

_____
_____

Where can I express gratitude for my talents by sharing them? Is there a place where I feel called to take more of a leadership role, or someone that I can support in their effort to gain greater self-mastery?

_____
_____
_____

A HERO IS NO BRAVER THAN AN
ORDINARY MAN, BUT HE IS BRAVER
FIVE MINUTES LONGER.

RALPH WALDO EMERSON

BULGARIA

START
Istanbul

Kesan

Komotini

Meriana

Çanakkale
Troy

GREECE

TUR

Athens

Mycenae

Pylos
Sparti

CRETE

Eight o'Clock Line

BETWEEN A ROCK AND A HARD PLACE

Eight o'Clock Line

BETWEEN A ROCK AND A HARD PLACE

Is there some way for me to escape away from deadly Kharybdis, but yet fight the other one off?
ODYSSEUS

The goddess Circe has warned Odysseus that once he gets by the Sirens he will have to navigate his ship between two cliffs, each containing a separate terror. She tells him that to one side of the narrow passage, in a cavern halfway up the taller cliff, lives a female monster named Scylla.

She has twelve legs, all writhing, dangling down and six long swaying necks, a hideous head on each, each head barbed with a triple row of fangs, thickset, packed tight—armed to the hilt with black death! Holed up in the cavern's bowels from her waist down she shoots out her heads...wildly sweeping the reefs for dolphins, dog-fish or any bigger quarry.... No mariners yet can boast they've raced their ship past Scylla's lair without some

*mortal blow—with each of her six heads she snatches
up a man from the dark-prowed craft and whisks him
off. (XII:89–100)*

Circe tells Odysseus that just an arrow-shot away,
opposite, will be a shaggy fig tree on the lower cliff. Lurking below it is Kharybdis, a whirlpool that sucks down
the sea three times a day and then spews it up three times.
"May you not be there when she sucks down water," Circe
warns, "for not even the Earthshaker [Poseidon] could
rescue you out of that evil." (XII:106–107) She advises
Odysseus that in order to survive he must hug the cliff of
Scylla and relinquish six men to her rather than lose the
entire crew to Kharybdis.

Odysseus wants to know why he cannot fight off
the monster Scylla so he can save all his crew. In reply,
Circe teaches him this lesson: "Must you have battle in your
heart forever? The bloody toil of combat? Old contender,
will you not yield to the immortal gods? That nightmare
cannot die.... No power can fight her." (XII:116–120) Circe
tells Odysseus that the only tactic that will work is to flee.

After passing the Sirens, Odysseus and his men
hear the thunderous sound of booming waves. Terrified,
the men let their oars fly from their hands and the ship
lays dead in the water. Odysseus walks up and down the
ship, stopping by each man to hearten him. "Friends," he
says, "we're hardly strangers at meeting danger—and this
danger is no worse than what we faced when Cyclops
penned us up in his vaulted cave with crushing force! But
even from there my courage, my presence of mind and
tactics saved us all." (XII:208–212)

"I saw their feet and hands from below, already lifted high above me, and they cried out to me,...the last time they ever did it, in heart's sorrow," laments Odysseus.

Odysseus then gives his crew explicit instructions to steer away from the whirlpool. But he tells them nothing of the monster Scylla "for fear the men would panic, desert their oars" and hide. (XII:224–225) Even though Circe has warned Odysseus that it will do no good to arm himself against Scylla, he dons his armor and grabs a long spear in each hand.

The eyes of every man are fixed on the dread whirlpool when suddenly, from the other side, Scylla snatches away six of the men, "the best of them for strength and hands' work," Odysseus says. "I saw their feet and hands from below, already lifted high above me, and they cried out to me,...the last time they ever did it, in heart's sorrow." (XII:246, 248–250) Scylla carries the six men up to her high, craggy cave and devours them at its entrance. Of all the incidents Odysseus has witnessed, the sight of these men reaching out to him is the worst, and it wrenches his heart to the quick.

TERRIFYING MONSTERS AS SYMBOLS

Fantasy and mythology provide clues about the monsters that lurk in our unconscious mind. Somewhere in the psyche is the reality behind these experiences. They are not created out of nothing. Perhaps the monsters come out of rebellion or a sense of injustice, frustration, anxiety, emotional tyranny, or another emotion or attitude that we experience when we refuse to surrender the ego, to let go, to follow our mentors or to follow our inner wisdom.

In the course of his trials Odysseus also encounters various feminine beings, whether women, goddesses or monsters. Some of these are beneficent and nurturing; others are terrifying and murderous. On a symbolic level, the terrors Scylla and Kharybdis can be understood as two guises of the mother-goddess that slays her children so that some portion of the self can transcend itself and become the higher self.

But whether Odysseus encounters physical beasts or Homer is using the symbolism of these beasts to describe various elements of the unconscious mind does not matter. What matters to us is how we relate to the elements of our unconscious. Our responses will provide us with clues as to where we go from here in our personal odyssey.

Moving forward with courage

In his encounter with Scylla and Kharybdis, Odysseus learns some painful but enduring lessons. On the positive side, he is meticulous and disciplined. Because he carries out Circe's instructions precisely, he succeeds in getting past this double bind with most of his crew still alive. He also displays mastery over his emotions. He does not let anxiety overtake him, nor does he let his emotions get out of control.

In this episode we also see that anxiety and fear of failure can lead to paralysis, an inability to act. This is what happens to the crew. Upon hearing the thundering roar of Kharybdis, the men freeze with fear, thinking the whirlpool will suck them down. In this state of terror, they throw their oars down and the ship stands still. To get his men and ship moving again, Odysseus must keep his own emotions and fear in check while also helping his crew members regain the courage to move forward in spite of their fear.

Odysseus has wisely refrained from telling his companions about Scylla, the danger that lurks on the other side of the ship. Now, to prevent them from panicking again and freezing within Scylla's reach, he focuses their attention on the whirlpool. This again shows discernment, for Circe has warned him of what could result from stopping beside Scylla's rock: "If you...waste time there, I fear she will make another outrush...and snatch away once more the same number of men." (XII:121–124) In other words, if we allow fear or panic to stop us from acting, we may be consumed by it.

VICTIMS CANNOT BE HEALED

Circe warns Odysseus that it is not possible to go beyond Scylla without paying the price she exacts. When he tells Circe that he would rather put up a good fight against Scylla than see six of his men die, she chides him: "Must you have battle in your heart forever?" In other words: "Must you always believe that the best way to deal with circumstances is to fight them?" In effect, she tells him: "Sometimes you just have to yield."

Sometimes there is no way to get out of our troubles, no way to move beyond our present circumstances, except to go through them. We call this being "between a rock and a hard place." That is exactly what is happening to Odysseus in this episode. He has to sail between two crags, steep rugged cliffs. He is literally between a rock (Scylla) and a hard place (Kharybdis), caught between two undesirable alternatives; and if he escapes one, he will fall into the hands of the other.

Odysseus passes another test of character in that he does not dwell on his losses but moves on. He does not criticize himself for not being able to save the six men who are eaten by Scylla. He had considered how he might save all his crew—the ideal situation. But when Circe assures him that he cannot, he accepts the reality of the situation and does not hold on to a false drive for perfection. Striving for perfection can be beneficial as long as we avoid falling into the trap of criticizing ourselves for missing the mark. Odysseus does not dwell on his losses and neither should we. He accepts the pain and is greatly saddened by it, but he moves on.

We are all dealing with circumstances that may be the result of our past actions. But if we can view challenging circumstances as an opportunity to balance our accounts with life or to learn an important lesson or, perhaps, to accept the hand life deals us and move forward with grace and equanimity, we will be less tempted to smart with a sense of injustice. Free will gives us an opportunity to make new choices with every thought, every feeling, every action.

When painful and challenging circumstances come our way, it can be very difficult not to say, "Why is this happening to me? It just isn't fair!" Grieving is a necessary part of coming to terms with deeply painful losses. And yet, rather than feeling that someone has been unjust to us or that life has dealt us an unfair blow, perhaps we can see the situation as an opportunity to wrestle with some aspect of ourselves or to make things right. Holding onto grief or to grudges does not heal our emotional wounds; it turns us into victims, and victims cannot be healed.

If we have nurtured a sense of injustice, we may be grappling with unresolved anger. Beneath anger we often find deep hurt. Anger can creep in from various angles, making inroads into our being that prevent us from being a citadel of strength and balance. A few of the guises of anger are apathy, agitation, aggravation, annoyance, accusation, argumentation and aggression.

The key to overcoming anger and its various manifestations is to look for the underlying issue and work to resolve that. It may take fierce dedication to get to the bottom of it, but when we do, we will see the anger dissolve also, because we will no longer be using it to protect ourselves from the hurt. As we move beyond the sense of injustice and resolve the underlying anger, we will also be resolving the deep hurt or other core issue that is beneath it.

PROBLEMS ARE SPRINGBOARDS TO GROWTH

Since emotional pain does not feel good, we may try to ignore our problems. We may procrastinate or fill our lives with so many activities that we do not have any time to stop and think about the pain or do anything to relieve it. Many of us, when we see emotional pain coming, tend to run the other way. If we are hurt, we may become embittered or close our hearts.

Wayne Muller, author of *Legacy of the Heart*, said that due to an injury, he has a headache every day. He said that for the first two years after the injury, he was very angry about having been dealt the "injustice" of chronic pain. He was frustrated because he could not find the right doctor, the right drug, the right acupuncturist that would take his pain away.

But he learned to distinguish between pain and suffering. Everybody has pain, he says, but suffering comes from the way you relate to the pain that you are given in this life. Muller says: "Only after going through the entire yellow pages did I come to the conclusion that, hey, suffering is part of the deal.... Then it stopped being suffering, and now it's just pain. There's a big difference."[9]

To grow spiritually takes a conscious choice to meet our problems head on and to use them as a springboard to spiritual and psychological growth. As Benjamin Franklin said, "Those things that hurt, instruct." And so it is that those who are wise learn not to dread but rather to welcome problems.

Eight o'Clock Line

TESTS OF JUSTICE

STRENGTHS	WEAKNESSES
has a sense of life's justice; accepts what "just is"	has a sense of injustice; feels victimized
mastery over emotions	masked or unresolved anger
analytical, meticulous, cautious	"analysis paralysis"; fearful, apprehensive
systematic, methodical, efficient, practical	intolerant, inflexible, stuck in mentally "fixing" everything
strives for a high standard; discriminating	overly critical, anxious; fears failure; may feel guilty
disciplined, reliable, dutiful, dedicated	works obsessively; narrow outlook

WHO AM I?
EIGHT O'CLOCK LINE: JUSTICE

Take a moment to think about justice in your life. Reflect on the chart of strengths and weaknesses and use it to evaluate your expressions of justice. Later in this chapter, you will have an opportunity to map your strategy for turning weaknesses into strengths.

What are my greatest strengths in relation to justice?

_____
_____
_____

What are my greatest weaknesses in relation to justice, especially in reaction to perceived injustice? Have I at times been a victim?

_____
_____
_____

Thus far in my life, how have I handled challenges involving aspects of justice? Would I handle any of those situations differently now? How?

_____
_____
_____

What can I learn about myself and justice from Odysseus' experience?

_____
_____
_____

Winning Strategies
EIGHT O'CLOCK LINE: JUSTICE

CALM YOUR EMOTIONS. Odysseus learns in this episode that it is not always the better part of wisdom to fight. When we struggle, feel anxious and resist pain, we tend to increase the struggle, the anxiety, the pain. Emotional extremes cannot help a difficult situation. Odysseus' men learn that they must not get stuck, paralyzed with fear. To an extent, the sense of struggle creates the struggle. In dangerous and critical situations, keep your emotions calm and steady.

If you keep moving forward, the movement itself will help you eventually break free from emotional extremes to get to the other side of the experience.

PAY THE PRICE AND MOVE ON. When you are stuck in a situation that you do not like and you cannot seem to surrender it, remember the lesson Odysseus learns with Scylla and Kharybdis: Sometimes there is no way out of your troubles except to go through them. Odysseus grieves his lost companions, feels grateful that most of his men were spared, and moves on. Had he stopped to fight the hand he was dealt, he might have lost all his men. Circe's warning is wise counsel:

Sometimes the only way to pass between a rock and a hard place is to yield, pay the price, count your blessings, and move forward.

WHEN PAIN IS INEVITABLE, ACCEPT IT AS YOUR TEACHER. Since emotional pain does not feel good, many of us try to ignore the problems that caused it. Alternatively, we may procrastinate or fill our lives with so many activities that we do not have time to stop and think about the pain or the underlying problems. In fact, if we even get a hint that pain is coming we may run the other way.

Instead of trying to avoid the pain that sometimes accompanies opportunities for growth, let it come to the surface and be transformed. You do not need to keep it sealed inside, where it may become a much greater burden to you. Pain is uncomfortable. Pain is hard. But pain is not bad; it is inevitable.

Pain opens us up to possibilities we would not recognize in any other way.

FORGIVE YOURSELF FOR YOUR PAST MISTAKES. When Odysseus makes a mistake, he learns from the experience and moves on. If your past mistakes revolve in your mind like a motion picture, this is a sign that you need to forgive yourself. Instead of feeling guilty about what you did or neglected to do, quietly put your attention on correcting it to the best of your ability. We have all stumbled and fallen, and we are all still worthy. Let us forgive our past and move on.

When old scenes come up, imagine them being consumed in forgiveness until the images disappear from your mind. If you desire, create a ritual: Write a note expressing regret and releasing the situation, then light a fire in a fireplace and burn the note. As the paper goes up in flames and turns to ash, let the sense of guilt and self-condemnation also be consumed.

Forgive yourself for past actions, learn the lesson and move on.

USE YOUR LEADERSHIP SKILLS TO INSPIRE AND SUPPORT OTHERS. Leading others takes momentum, energy and an ability to keep things moving forward. When members of a team get fearful or discouraged, as Odysseus' crew did, a good leader will assess whether the goal or task is realistic and achievable. If it is, they will inspire and support the team, helping them to regain their vision and confidence, encouraging their belief in their ability and worth.

Even in dire circumstances, where the goal seems impossible, a capable leader will move forward with visible courage that is contagious. And this, in the end, may bring forth miraculous results. No matter what outer role you play, you can inspire and support others and let them know that they can do it, that they can achieve their goal.

Using leadership skills, you can help people of every age, even very young children, to believe they can make a positive difference in the world and in the lives of others.

WHERE AM I GOING?
EIGHT O'CLOCK LINE: JUSTICE

As you reflect on the following questions, you may find it helpful to review the various aspects of justice in the chart on p. 192 and "The Stuff Heroes Are Made Of" on pp. 4–5, as well as the Winning Strategies. Using the questions below, map out a strategy to apply the insights you've gained.

In the tests of justice presented by my current life circumstances, how can I use my strengths constructively?

_____

_____

How can I turn any weakness I may have into an expression of justice that I can claim as a new strength? Do I have any painful experiences that I can heal by using them as a springboard to new growth?

_____

_____

Are there ways I can use what I have learned from difficult experiences to support others going through similar situations?

_____

_____

Where can I apply a high standard and attention to detail in a self-disciplined way to move forward with my mission in life?

_____

_____

_____

OUT OF SUFFERING HAVE EMERGED
THE STRONGEST SOULS; THE MOST MASSIVE
CHARACTERS ARE SEARED WITH SCARS.

ANONYMOUS

Nine o'Clock Line

TESTING THE METTLE

Nine o'Clock Line

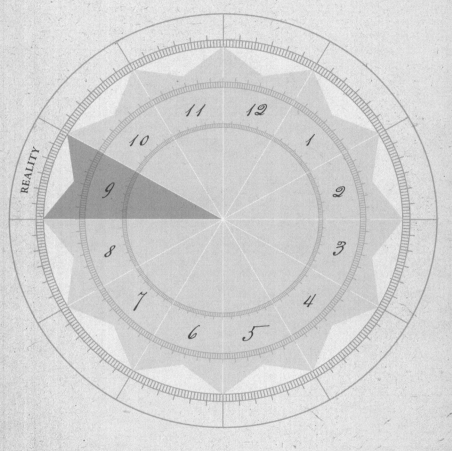

TESTING THE METTLE

*I saw then what evil the divinity had in mind
for us, and so I spoke aloud to him...: "Eurylochos,
I am only one man. You force me to it. But come
then all of you, swear a strong oath to me."*

ODYSSEUS

After their passage between Scylla and Kharybdis, Odysseus and his crew approach the lush, green island of the sun god, Helios. Both the prophet Teiresias and the goddess Circe have given Odysseus stern warning to avoid the island, for the cattle and sheep that pasture there are sacred. "There is no giving birth among them," said Circe, "nor do they ever die away.... If you do harm them, then I testify to the destruction of your ship and your companions." (XII:130–131, 139–140)

Odysseus conveys this warning to his bone-weary shipmates and urges them to row past the shores of the beautiful island. He attempts to hearten them, saying: "Listen to me, my comrades, brothers in hardship...: Time again they told me to shun this island of the Sun, the joy of man. Here, they warned, the worst disaster awaits us. Row straight past these shores—race our black ship on!" (XII:271–276)

But there is mutiny in the air. The crew cannot eat or sleep while sailing, so they want to go ashore. They are spent after the harrowing encounters with Scylla and Kharybdis. Odysseus' second-in-command, Eurylochos, complains bitterly:

> *Are you flesh and blood, Odysseus, to endure more than a man can? Do you never tire? God, look at you, iron is what you're made of. Here we all are, half dead with weariness, falling asleep over the oars, and you say "No landing"—no firm island earth where we could make a quiet supper. No: pull out to sea, you say, with night upon us—just as before, but wandering now, and lost. Sudden storms can rise at night and swamp ships without a trace....*
>
> *I say do as the hour demands and go ashore before black night comes down. We'll make our supper alongside, and at dawn put out to sea. (XII:279–287, 291–293)*

Feeling outnumbered, Odysseus agrees to stop overnight if all the men vow that they will not harm any of Helios' herds but only eat the food that Circe has put on board for them. The men all swear their strong oath that they will not "in evil and reckless action...slaughter any ox or sheep." (XII:300–301) After they beach the ship, the winds turn against them and they cannot set sail again for an entire month. Their food supply runs out and they

Led by Eurylochos, Odysseus' companions round up the sacred cattle of Helios.

are forced to live on fish and birds. They grow lean with hunger.

In desperation one day, Odysseus goes off to pray in solitude to the gods, hoping one of them will show him a course to sail on. "But what they did," he says, "was to shed a sweet sleep on my eyelids." (XII:338) While Odysseus sleeps, Eurylochos encourages the men to break their vow. Otherwise, he claims, they will die of famine. Then Eurylochos pleads:

Come, we'll cut out the noblest of these cattle for sacrifice to the gods who own the sky; and once at home...we'll build a costly temple and adorn it with every beauty for the Lord of Noon. But if he flares up over his heifers lost, wishing our ship destroyed, and if the gods make cause with him, why, then I say: Better open your lungs to a big sea once for all than waste to skin and bones on a lonely island. (XII:343–351)

Odysseus awakes and heads back. He smells the roasting meat and is horrified. Though he takes the men to task, the deed is done and he can do nothing about it. Soon, Odysseus says, "the gods began to show forth portents before us. The skins crawled, and the meat that was stuck on the spits bellowed, both roast and raw." (XII:394–396) Nonetheless, the men feast on their kill for six days. Odysseus alone abstains.

The sun god Helios is enraged that his cattle have been killed. He gives Zeus an ultimatum: "Restitution or penalty they shall pay—and pay in full—or I go down forever to light the dead men in the underworld." (XII:381–383) Rather than risk never again seeing sunlight in the world of gods and living men, Zeus promises justice.

At last the contrary winds cease and Odysseus and his crew set sail. Before long, a howling wind tears down the mast, then Zeus hurls a white-hot lightning bolt into the ship, breaking it into splinters. All the men except Odysseus are killed. "My men were thrown in the water, and bobbing like sea crows they were washed away on the running waves all around the black ship, and the god took away their homecoming." (XII:417–420)

Odysseus creates a makeshift raft from the mast and keel and drifts all night on the sea. When the sun rises, he finds himself once again between the deadly whirlpool of Kharybdis and the monster Scylla. Just then Kharybdis sucks in the water and pulls down his raft. Odysseus heaves himself up and clutches the bough of the fig tree that overhangs the whirlpool. He clings to the branch "like a bat," waiting for Kharybdis to spit up his raft.

Late in the day, the whirlpool spews up the water and his raft. Odysseus lets go of the branch, drops into the waves and scrambles onto the raft. He rows with his hands through the strait and passes the monster Scylla undetected. Attributing his safe passage to Zeus, Odysseus says: "Never could I have passed her had not the Father of gods and men, this time, kept me from her eyes." (XII:445–446)

For nine days and nights, Odysseus drifts alone on the open sea.

STANDING FIRM UNDER PRESSURE

In this trial on the island of Helios, Odysseus learns that allegiance to the harmony and law of his inner being is more important than compromising in order to maintain temporary harmony with his crew. He handles the challenging and subtle circumstances of this test by giving rein to his crew members' desires and logic instead of holding firmly to what he knows is for their higher good. By doing so, he exposes them to a fatal temptation.

The episode highlights a classic dilemma in which relationships and the law are at stake: Should Odysseus give in to his exhausted, hungry men or force them to keep sailing in order to protect them from temptation? The better choice may seem obvious in retrospect, but this is a subtle test. Could Odysseus have used his well-honed skill as an orator to paint so unmistakable a picture of the impending disaster that the men would willingly have raced past the island? Could he have inspired them to keep on? Or would they have mutinied? We do not know.

Although Odysseus conveys the warning of Teiresias and Circe to his crew members, he does not stand firm when his crew side with Eurylochos. He will pay dearly for the temporary harmony he purchases through this compromise.

After being stuck on the island for a month, Eurylochos again persuades the men with his logic even while he reminds them of the price they may pay for their indulgence. The men give in to their rumbling stomachs and forsake their oath. This test marks a dividing of the way: The men fail and Odysseus succeeds. They die and he lives.

We may be tempted to feel sympathy for the crew members, and indeed, the loss of life is a tragedy. But also remember that on a symbolic level the men are aspects of Odysseus. They represent his lesser self, his worldly desires and appetites. In one sense, this entire episode could be understood as an instructive dream. And if it is not a dream, consider that Odysseus, too, is lean with hunger, yet he survives without partaking of the forbidden cattle. The stark reality is that we cannot forsake our allegiance to our inner oath, our integrity, without paying a price.

At a certain point in our voyage of self-discovery, we will each face a trial by fire, a test of our ability to choose what is right, to stand firm under pressure. The moment when the "bill collector" comes to demand payment is often the most inconvenient time—just when we are about to launch a business or have a wonderful marriage or enjoy a good situation in life or go home to Ithaca. When that bill collector comes to our door, we have no choice but to go back and pick up the pieces of what we left hanging so that we can again move forward.

THE RAZOR'S EDGE

In this trial, Odysseus and his crew members are dealing with reality and unreality, and each has to determine which is which. To embrace reality is to renounce unreality, and at times the distinction between them may be a razor's edge. As this episode demonstrates, it can be very difficult to know when to bend with grace and when to stand firm in saying no to others.

To his credit, Odysseus understands and honors the cultural codes of his time, laws and traditions that the ancient Greeks believed were instituted and sponsored by the gods. He obeys the injunction not to eat the sacred cattle of Helios. But his men do not share the same respect for the law. By violating their oath, they commit one of the most serious of sins for the Greeks: the sin of *hubris*. Hubris is the pride, ambition and overconfidence that leads a hero to ignore the warnings of the gods or to disregard established moral codes.

To the ancient Greeks, *hubris* was a form of wanton arrogance that often caused the downfall of great men. In effect, Odysseus' men choose to preserve their lower self rather than obey their higher self and the higher law. Once we know the law, we are accountable to obey it. The men may lack faith in the order of the universe, or perhaps they do not believe that they have within themselves the fortitude and ability to pass any test of character that will come to them.

To take an example from a familiar situation: Parents find it very difficult at times to say no to their children, especially when the children are not yet able to understand the reason they cannot have what they want. And yet, if we do not stand firm and do not require our children to stand firm in what we know or believe is right, their ego can grow bigger and bigger.

This pattern, if allowed to continue until it reaches a critical point, could eventually lead to where, in place of an inner knowing and an inner contact with the higher self, the child's journey through life takes him far astray into the realm of the ego, a realm where there is no true reality, no true love, no true wisdom, no true power—in short, a life without genuine fulfillment.

To raise responsible individuals, parents must teach even the youngest children to make their primary allegiance to higher principles rather than to momentary whims or playmates. Over time, through careful and loving instruction, children learn that obedience to higher principles maintains a higher harmony that also, ultimately, keeps harmony with others.

COMPROMISE

To find fulfillment takes understanding and following the rules and principles that govern relationships. One of the challenges we face in this regard is to honor our own needs while addressing the needs of others. Like Odysseus in this episode, we may be tempted to focus on what others want. To please them, we may say what they want to hear. We may make certain decisions so that others will like us. We may be tempted to seek harmony at the human level rather than stay tethered to a principle we know is right. In other words, we may be tempted to compromise rather than seek true balance.

Odysseus tries to preserve the harmony of his crew even though he knows it might lead to no good. He knows that they can be reckless. After all, these are the men who, earlier in the voyage, opened the bag of winds that sent the ship flying back to its starting point. These are the men who walked into Circe's trap and were turned into pigs. Can he really trust them now?

In the episode with the bag containing the contrary winds, Odysseus did not entrust his crew members with the knowledge of its contents. Had he imparted that knowledge to them, they might have made a better choice. But would they have believed him? That would remain to be seen. To Odysseus' credit in this episode on Helios' island, he trusts his men sufficiently to leave them in the midst of temptation while he goes apart to pray for a solution. In this instance, the men do not honor that trust.

When someone else's actions are endangering our own identity, we can choose to draw healthy boundaries. It may take some practice until we are able to take a balanced stand for ourselves while still extending ourselves lovingly to others. But we can learn to see situations through the eyes of reality instead of projecting what we wish were the case.

In this episode, Odysseus wishes and hopes that his men can resist the temptation to kill the sacred cattle. But this is not realistic. And in his heart, Odysseus perhaps knows this, knows that his gut feeling was right—to keep on moving and not to stop at the island of Helios. It is good to uphold others by believing in them and supporting them. But it is dangerous to be so blinded to reality that we sacrifice our own progress out of sympathy or to keep the peace.

TRIAL BY FIRE

At this stage of his journey, Odysseus is tested in the intense fires of love, the trial by fire. This testing has also been likened to a dark night. For Odysseus it is, literally, both. Zeus's fiery lightning bolt signals the beginning of the trial by fire. It destroys the ship and brings death to the crew members. Odysseus is all alone now, bereft of all external support.

One way to see this experience is that, through the loss of his ship and all of his crew, Odysseus is stripped of the substance of his lesser self, his ego self, that which is not part of his reality. With his crew gone, Odysseus can no longer rely on them or on his own human craftiness. He has nowhere to turn but within himself. All he can depend on now is what is real—his higher self, his inner being, his inner reality.

Literally and symbolically, Odysseus enters the dark night. Utterly alone, he floats on his makeshift raft through the long night. The following day he must once again pass between Scylla and Kharybdis. When he survives his harrowing encounter with the whirlpool and then rows past the monster Scylla unseen, he does not attribute his salvation to his own cleverness; he believes that Zeus has saved him. For Odysseus, this is a turning point.

The experience reinforces for Odysseus the lesson that in order to reach home, he must be utterly humble. In return for his obedience to the cultural codes and higher laws, and by continuing to give his all, Odysseus has merited this providence.

As this episode shows, though there will be times in our soul's odyssey when we feel utterly alone, none of us makes it in life without support and nurturing somewhere along the way. To pass tests of character takes giving our all, following the inner law of our being, and also, at times, having the support of others.

If we take the *Odyssey* symbolically, in this episode on the island of Helios, Odysseus is forced to let go of everything that is not real, everything that no longer serves him on his journey to wholeness. In the process of letting go, he is liberated from the parts of himself that are sabotaging him—those rebellious, disobedient and reckless parts. As noted earlier, when we transform the negative aspects of our being into their positive counterparts, we liberate the energy that has been tied up in those patterns.

Reflect on Odysseus' fortitude. He accepts every trial and learns from it. He quickly figures out his vulnerabilities and what it will take to survive. He has a heart for any fate. He knows that his mentor, the goddess Athena, is a fierce teacher. He accepts what comes to him and he keeps going. He makes the best of difficult circumstances.

Let us not fool ourselves. As this episode shows, growth and change and letting go can be a painful process.

To become our higher self takes vision, endurance, and hard work. But when we have submitted to life's trials, we will also experience joy. If we forgo the voyage—the endurance, the hard work, the pain, the suffering, the inner depths of soul wrenching—then we will never know the brightness and the joy that awaits us.

Why would we want to undergo a trial by fire? For one thing, the stripping action of the fires of love serves a purpose. It tears down the foundations of our life so we can build on a better foundation. Think of those, for example, who lose their home and all their possessions in a natural disaster. This is a very painful experience. And yet a significant number of people who have lived through such a loss will say that the disaster was a defining moment in their life, for in losing "everything," they realize that they still have what really matters to them.

As we are seeing in our journey with Odysseus, life will test our strengths and weaknesses to determine if we are ready to shed the snakeskin of our former self and embrace greater wholeness. Until Odysseus forsakes his former ways and balances his inner masculine and inner feminine, he will not complete his journey. Once Odysseus achieves a sufficient level of balance, the gods themselves direct his passage. As we replace what hinders us with what strengthens and supports us, we will find ourselves making progress in our journey.

Sometimes the trial by fire is a summing up in which we are dealing with the return of the energy we have sent out. But it can instead be the testing of our mettle. There is no reason to fear the trial by fire. As in Odysseus' case, this trial comes when we can withstand the purging that is necessary in order to receive a greater increment of fire, of energy, in our being. Like the mythical phoenix that rises from the ashes reborn, we are destined to emerge from the fire transformed. But we must meet fire with fire. We need to bank the fire in our being to meet the oncoming fire of love.

The trial by fire does not necessarily happen all at once, nor will its outer appearance be the same in each case. It can come in increments. It may come as the loss of a spouse or a close friend or a child. Our home may burn down or be flooded. We may lose our job or our livelihood. We may be stricken with a long-term illness or have an accident. When it comes, then suddenly we have to redefine ourselves. Without spouse or friend or job, who are we?

When we go through a trial by fire, we are stripped of something old so we can open to something new. As Kahlil Gibran wrote: "Your pain is the breaking of the shell that encloses your understanding. Even as the stone of the fruit must break, that its heart may stand in the sun, so must you know pain."[10] Pain opens the outworn shell so that the seed of our higher potential can grow.

Here again comes the universal mother-goddess for the testing of our souls. Like the goddess Athena, the universal mother-goddess is the personification of primal elements. This force appears in a multitude of guises, for the possibilities of the matter creation are innumerable. The goddess comes swooping down in the guise of a Scylla to make us forget our lesser self. Like Circe, she pokes fun at our idiosyncrasies and at those little sacred parts of ourselves that we would *not* be without. And all of a sudden, when we come to our senses and are willing to find joy in a quiet wisdom, we realize that we have been stripped of one more element of the lesser consciousness that we did not need.

If the goddess wants to use demons to test us, she will not hold back the hordes of darkness but will allow them to come trampling like a herd of elephants upon us so that we can find out where we are vulnerable. Just when we think we need her most, she is not there—as if to say, like Athena in the *Odyssey*, "I will not come near you. Go and fight the battle yourself." Through the testing, the soul consciousness is ejected from the symbolic womb and must fend for itself as an identity. Those who, like Odysseus, survive the ordeal with grace, come out wiser for having endured.

Are we ready to accept the goddess, this universal force, as our teacher?

When all the obstacles and ogres have been overcome, the ultimate adventure is the mythical union of the triumphant hero, the outer masculine stripped of the lesser self, with the queen-mother-wife-sister-goddess, the inner feminine. This union represents the marriage of the soul with its inner polarity. The hero unites with his inner feminine; the heroine unites with her inner masculine.

ANCHORING YOUR INSIGHTS

Nine o'Clock Line

TESTS OF REALITY

STRENGTHS	WEAKNESSES
tethered to inner reality, true to the inner law of being	distorted sense of reality; self-deceived
never compromises higher principles	indecisive, passive, compromising
harmonious; plays fair in relationships	peace at any price; dependent or codependent
diplomatic, tactful; good mediator	changeable, insincere; says what others want to hear
cooperative, helpful; sensitive to needs of others	focuses inappropriately on needs of others
even-tempered, calm	explosive temper, unstable emotions

WHO AM I?

NINE O'CLOCK LINE: REALITY

Take a moment to think about reality in your life. Reflect on the chart of strengths and weaknesses and use it to evaluate your expressions of reality. Later in this chapter, you will have an opportunity to map your strategy for turning weaknesses into strengths.

What are my greatest strengths in relation to discerning the reality at play between the inner law of my being and my interactions with others?

_____

_____

What are my greatest weaknesses in relation to reality, especially concerning relationships and values?

_____

_____

_____

Thus far in my life, how have I handled challenges involving aspects of reality? Would I handle any of those situations differently now? How?

_____

_____

_____

What can I learn about myself and reality from Odysseus' experience? Have I faced a trial by fire in my life?

_____

_____

_____

WINNING STRATEGIES
NINE O'CLOCK LINE: REALITY

FIND YOUR INNER REALITY AND HOLD FIRM TO IT. From Odysseus' trials, we can learn something about what to expect on our soul's odyssey. We will all at some point come to a difficult crossroads where we feel utterly alone on our voyage of self-discovery. The better prepared you are for these tests, the more likely you are to sail through them victoriously. Work at finding your inner reality and hold firm to it every step of your journey.

Like the refiner's fire, the trial by fire strips from you only the dross. Because it burns up whatever is not part of your inner reality and leaves intact the gold of your real self, you have no reason to fear a trial by fire.

You are destined to emerge from the fire transformed, but you must be ready for it and claim it.

CULTIVATE DECISIVENESS. Teens tend to move in a crowd. They dress alike. They talk alike. They look to each other for approval and acceptance. In many cases youth feel a need to be like their peers because of their uncertainty about themselves. They are still pondering life's questions: "Who am I? How will I express myself? How will I bring myself to become the person that I will finally be when I become an adult?" Sadly, if they do stand apart from the crowd, they may at times suffer the unkindness or rejection of their peers.

Sometimes, in both youth and adults, when we see ourselves wavering when we need to make a decision, it may be because we can see both sides of a question and can appreciate the value of each. We learn from Odysseus' experience in this episode that it is the better part of wisdom to trust in our own gut feelings and intuition and then act on them.

Rather than avoiding issues or just going along with others, go within your heart and be decisive about what you know you need to do.

LIVE IN INTEGRITY. Sometimes we take our blessings for granted. If we live a reasonably good life, we may tend to give ourselves some slack. We may ignore or indulge in little transgressions. We may think: "I'll just take a few supplies from work, take them home for my kids." Or "It will not matter if I make a few personal phone calls on the company bill." Or "I won't tell the cashier that she just gave me ten dollars too much change."

The problem with crossing the line—for instance, cheating on rules, breaking laws, or forsaking a promise to a friend—is that we think that these little transgressions will not matter. But there are consequences to whatever we do. What we send out returns to us.

If you make a commitment, keep your commitment. If you have fallen short, above all do not condemn yourself. Instead, dedicate yourself to truth and integrity. If you wronged someone, ask for their forgiveness, forgive yourself and move on. Do whatever is necessary and possible to make amends, to bring the situation back into balance and resolution.

The more you live in integrity, the more wind you will have in your sail to reach your goals.

TO THINE OWN SELF BE TRUE. If we focus too much on others we may ignore our own needs and goals. If we do not maintain healthy boundaries, we may become depressed or angry or even sick, because we have denied some part of ourselves. In *Hamlet*, Shakespeare captured the antidote. In this scene Polonius, the king's advisor, is advising his son Laertes: "This above all: to thine own self be true, and it must follow, as the night the day, thou canst not then be false to any man."[11]

As you move through life and learn from your experiences, you may find your friendships changing. Old friends may mature along with you and you will find your relationships with them growing richer and more rewarding. Other friends may pass into a relative background as your paths diverge. It can be painful to say goodbye to an old friendship, lifestyle or job that can no longer support you in reaching for your destiny. Yet any of these may be keeping you from attracting more supportive relationships, situations and opportunities. Have faith that you will make new friends who are more supportive of your soul's odyssey.

Even if you leave behind outworn friendships, it is better to be true to yourself than to go around being a mirror for other people.

BALANCE THE NEED FOR HARMONY WITH A CLOSE LOOK AT REALITY. Sometimes we desperately want everything to work out right. We want to be a peacemaker. We may have an out-of-balance desire for harmonious relationships or we may put our need for companionship above everything else. As a result, we may overlook someone's faults or their true motives. If you are faced with the tendency to deny realities, ask yourself, or if you need a reality check, you can ask a tried and true friend: "What is really going on here?"

If things are not right in your life, take time for soul searching, because your very best friend is your higher self. You may wish to attend a retreat with others, or you might prefer to spend time alone to achieve clarity and a better understanding of what is really real.

Do whatever it takes to have clear vision and bring yourself into harmony with your inner reality.

WHERE AM I GOING?
NINE O'CLOCK LINE: REALITY

As you reflect on the following questions, you may find it helpful to review the various aspects of reality in the chart on p. 217 and "The Stuff Heroes Are Made Of" on pp. 4–5, as well as the Winning Strategies. Using the questions below, map out a strategy to apply the insights you've gained.

In the tests of reality presented by my current life circumstances, how can I use my strengths constructively?

_____

How can I turn any weakness I may have into an expression of reality that I can claim as a new strength?

_____

What steps can I take to further explore and strengthen my awareness of my inner reality, the inner law of my being that guides me when I make decisions?

_____

_____

Are there any areas of my life where I need to examine what is real, whether in a relationship, a job or an activity, and make changes in harmony with my inner reality?

_____

_____

Am I prepared for a trial by fire? What would it take for me to be able to face an experience like this?

_____

_____

IF I WERE DROPPED OUT OF A PLANE
INTO THE OCEAN AND TOLD THE NEAREST
LAND WAS A THOUSAND MILES AWAY,
I'D STILL SWIM.

ABRAHAM MASLOW

Ten o'Clock Line

A TEMPERED SOUL

FOLLOWING
THE ROUTE OF
ODYSSEUS

Ten o'Clock Line

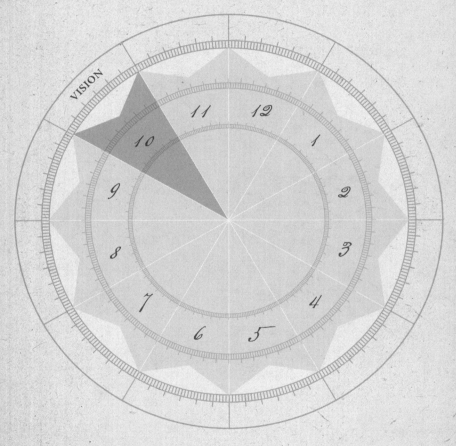

VISION

11 12

10 1

9 2

8 3

7 4

6 5

KALYPSO'S SEDUCTION

A TEMPERED SOUL

Nevertheless I long...to travel home and see
the dawn of my return. And if a god will wreck me
yet again on the wine-dark sea, I can bear that too,
with a spirit tempered to endure.

ODYSSEUS

In the dead of night, after nine days of drifting on the open sea on a makeshift raft, Odysseus, utterly alone, is cast upon the shore of a remote island that is home to the goddess Kalypso.

Kalypso rescues Odysseus, cares for him, feeds him, and caresses him. The goddess wants him to remain with her forever, and works "ever with soft and flattering words...to charm him to forget Ithaca." (I:56–57) She offers Odysseus immortality if he will be her husband, but he never consents. He yearns deeply for his homeland and all that it holds for him. But without a ship and crew, and lacking tools with which to build a sturdy craft, he must remain Kalypso's captive.

*But when in the circling of the years that very year came
in which the gods had spun for him his time of homecoming to Ithaca, not even then was he free of his trials....*

*The sweet lifetime was draining out of him.... By
nights he would lie beside her, of necessity, in the hollow
caverns, against his will, by one who was willing, but
all the days he would sit upon the rocks, at the seaside,
breaking his heart in tears and lamentation and sorrow
as weeping tears he looked out over the barren water.*
(I:16–18, V:152–158)

The gods, all but Poseidon, pity Odysseus. At
last, while Poseidon is away, Athena pleads Odysseus'
case before the gods on Mt. Olympus. Zeus dispatches
the messenger-god Hermes to announce his command to
Kalypso: "Send him on his way with all speed. It is not appointed for him to die here, away from his people. It is still
his fate that he shall see his people and come back to his
house with the high roof and to the land of his fathers."
(V:112–115)

Upon hearing this pronouncement, Kalypso
shudders. She complains to Hermes that the gods are
hard-hearted, proving resentful whenever a goddess takes
a "mortal friend." She rails: "But it was I who saved him....
I fed him, loved him, sang that he should not die nor grow
old, ever, in all the days to come. But now there's no elud-
ing Zeus's will.... My counsel he shall have, and nothing
hidden, to help him homeward without harm." Hermes
warns her: "Thus you shall send him, then. And show
more grace in your obedience, or be chastised by Zeus."
(V:119–120, 130–138, 143–146)

Kalypso says to Odysseus, "Grieve no more....
I have pondered it, and I shall help you go."

Kalypso finds Odysseus on the seashore and announces that she will let him go. Wary, he makes her swear that this is not some new wickedness she is plotting against him. She swears sincere intent, then once more tempts him to stay with her: "If you could see it all, before you go—all the adversity you face at sea—you would stay here, and guard this house, and be immortal.... Can I be less desirable than [your wife] is: Less interesting? Less beautiful? Can mortals compare with goddesses in grace and form?" (V:206–213)

Poseidon's hurricane throws him from his raft. Odysseus says within himself, "Rag of man that I am, is this the end of me?"

Odysseus holds firm. He tactfully acknowledges that Kalypso's beauty surpasses that of Penelope's, then masterfully shifts the focus of his longing away from his wife. He tells Kalypso: "Each day I long for home, long for the sight of home. If any god has marked me out again for shipwreck, my tough heart can undergo it. What hardship have I not long since endured at sea, in battle! Let the trial come." (V:219–224)

Kalypso now does everything she can to help Odysseus prepare for his journey. She shows him where the best timber can be found. She gives him fine tools with which to build a raft and sail cloth to make the sails. Then the goddess bathes him and gives him a scented cloak. After telling him the stars to navigate by, she sees him off from her island.

Odysseus sets sail well supplied with food and wine. On his eighteenth day of sailing, the wrathful Poseidon spies him. Not yet finished with Odysseus, Poseidon whips up a hurricane that throws him from his raft. A sea nymph pities Odysseus and tells him to shed Kalypso's heavy cloak and instead tie the nymph's own immortal veil around his waist to protect him from drowning. Odysseus regains his raft momentarily until a great wave, a final assault by Poseidon, breaks up his raft and leaves him clinging to a single beam. He dons the nymph's veil and dives head first into the water, swimming hard.

Athena calms all the winds but one. Odysseus swims and drifts on the sea for two days. At dawn on the third day Athena guides him to the shore of an island. The waves are about to throw him onto "ragged rock-teeth and boulders" when again Athena comes to the rescue. Inspired by her, Odysseus seizes a reef with both hands and hangs on for dear life. A breaker's backwash hurls him out to sea once more. He prays fervently to the god of the river to have mercy on him. The river god draws him safely to shore at the river's mouth.

Odysseus is a battered man, "his very heart sick with salt water, and all his flesh...swollen." The skin is torn from his hands. Seawater is gushing from his mouth and nostrils. He collapses on the beach. Then, summoning his remaining strength, he tosses the nymph's veil back into the ocean and stumbles to a nearby wood. There he finds a womb-like shelter underneath two closely inter-woven bushes, a dense shrub and a wild olive, "close to the water in a conspicuous place." (V:454, 475–476) It will serve to shield him from both wild beasts and the elements.

> *Odysseus entered, and with his own hands heaped him a bed [of fallen leaves] to sleep on.... Long-suffering great Odysseus was happy, and lay down in the middle, and made a pile of leaves over him. As when a man buries a burning log in a black ash heap in a remote place in the country, where none live near as neighbors, and saves the seed of fire, having no other place to get a light from, so Odysseus buried himself in the leaves, and Athena shed a sleep on his eyes so as most quickly to quit him, by veiling his eyes, from the exhaustion of his hard labors." (V:481–482, 486–491)*

While Odysseus sleeps deeply, Athena arranges for his rescue. On this island Odysseus meets the Phaiakians, a people who are "near the gods in origin." Odysseus, ever the master storyteller, enchants then with riveting tales of his adventures and wins the admiration, compassion and good graces of this people. Athena inspires the Phaiaki-ans to honor Odysseus with lavish gifts of gold, bronze and textiles. Stowing these in the hull of the fast-running Phaiakian ship that will convey him across the sea, they bid Odysseus farewell. As the ship speeds him on toward his destiny, Odysseus, "a man with a mind like the gods for counsel," lies in a gentle, sweet sleep, "oblivious of all he had suffered." (V:35; XIII:89, 92) Odysseus is going home.

CAUGHT BETWEEN CONFLICTING DESIRES

There is more than one way to interpret Odysseus' seven-year trial on Kalypso's island. We can see Odysseus as being stuck in a trap of desire. Or we can see him as enduring through a long, dark night and finally breaking through to the other side. Yet again, we can see him as being caught between lower and higher desires.

Odysseus must evaluate his desires. At night he makes love to the goddess Kalypso and by day he sits on the beach crying and looking off into the sea. In this glyph, with its contrast of day and night, "night" represents Odysseus' lower, sensual desires while "day" represents his higher desire to reach home. Several times in the *Odyssey*, we read that it is Odysseus' destiny to reach home. What is keeping him from getting there?

If we take this episode literally, Odysseus appears to be wasting his life-force by overindulgence in sex; as a result, he becomes passive and weak. If we take it symbolically, Odysseus is channeling his energy into inordinate desires and so he has no energy left to fuel the desire that leads to his destiny. Odysseus wants to go home, yet he sits on the shore looking out into the distance instead of doing something about it. By channeling his energy into desires that are not in line with his vision, he does not have the verve to get up and go.

Alternatively, we can instead look at sex as a symbol of regeneration. In fact, issues of death and rebirth, destruction and regeneration are all at play in this pivotal episode. Odysseus remains with Kalypso for seven years. To the ancient Greeks, seven years symbolized a lifetime. It takes seven years for our bodies to renew themselves.

We could therefore interpret this episode to mean that Odysseus is going through a rebirth of sorts. Now, after a necessary period of recuperation and regeneration, he is evaluating and prioritizing his desires. Once he has freed himself from his lesser desires, he is reborn. Thus, when Zeus commands Kalypso to free Odysseus, Odysseus in fact seems like a new man. He is once again actively in control, firm about his goal and ready to take on the world.

The god Hermes, Zeus's message-bearer, can again be seen as representing the wisdom of the higher self. As this episode shows, it takes the intervention of the higher self, with its resolute will, to transform Odysseus' inordinate desires and indulgent emotions into the one-pointed passion that will move him forward.

The goddess Kalypso speaks of herself as compassionate and helpful. She saves Odysseus' life when he washes up on her shore but she uses her intense drive to overpower and manipulate him. Kalypso symbolizes stubborn, controlling possessiveness and the indulgence of inordinate desires. She detains Odysseus even though she knows that she is "no longer pleasing to him" and that his real desire lies elsewhere. Through her possessiveness she is causing him to "mourn" and his life essence to "fade away." (V:153–154, 160–161) Yet she stubbornly refuses to give him his freedom. On Kalypso's island paradise, Odysseus is suffering a slow death.

The name *Kalypso* comes from the Greek word meaning "to cover or conceal" (*kalyptein*), a word that shares the same Proto-Indo-European root (kel-) as the English word *hell*. Kalypso attempts to conceal, or eclipse, Odysseus' mission and destiny in order to satisfy her own inordinate desire. Only when Zeus commands her to let him go does she bring out the tools and resources Odysseus needs to build the craft that will carry him across the ocean.

TEMPTATION TO FORSAKE THE DREAM

Still another way of looking at this trial is that Odysseus is facing the Tempter—or, in this case, the Temptress. By appealing to his pride, Kalypso tempts Odysseus to forsake his dream of going home and his destiny. She tempts him to indulge in self-idolatry by seeing himself as a god. Kalypso seems the perfect Temptress for a hero like Odysseus. She lives on a utopian island, she is gorgeous, and she makes him an offer that would be hard to refuse: She wants to make him into a god who will live forever and never grow old.

Kalypso's offer of immortality is extremely rare. In Greek mythology only a few mortals attained immortality. To his credit, Odysseus resists. In remaining loyal to his dream of home, he displays tremendous endurance and staying power. A lesser man than Odysseus would have fallen for Kalypso's flattering offer.

A distorted desire for human immortality, or for eternal youth, is not uncommon in our own society today. Physical self-infatuation is a lure that can drive people to try just about anything to make their fifty-year-old bodies look and perform like a twenty-year-old body. They are looking for the magic pill, hormone treatment or gadget that will make it happen. Maintaining a healthy body is wise. But worshiping the body for the sake of the ego is another thing.

We might view this episode as Odysseus' enduring through a long, dark night as he sifts through his lower desires and his unconscious to clear himself of all that is preventing him from reaching his goal. The trial that began on the island of Helios with Odysseus being stripped of all his external support continues on Kalypso's island. Athena, Odysseus' guide and mentor, continues to remain out of sight.

Odysseus must first prove his mettle by showing that, come what may, he will not succumb to Kalypso's temptation. Only then does Athena enter the scene. Athena sees Odysseus wasting away on his island prison without hope of release. She begs her father, Zeus, to intercede. Why does Athena wait seven years? For one thing, Odysseus first has to balance some accounts and sift through his desires. He needs to overcome certain challenges on his own.

There are times in our odyssey when we just cannot make it without help. And yet, we cannot be truly successful if someone does everything for us or steps in too soon. We need to prime the pump and forge our own victories.

INTERNALIZING A HIGHER VISION

Vision is another pivotal issue in this trial. Odysseus has the clear vision he needs to see beyond Kalypso's seductive offer of immortality. He may recognize that her offer could only lead to an endless mortal existence. And so, although mortal life includes hardships and trials, he chooses his humanity and remains true to his goal and calling to return home.

Having internalized his higher vision, Odysseus sees and rejects selfishness, self-love and idolatry—traits that Kalypso embodies. These traits distort vision, blinding a person from seeing things as they really are or from seeing them through a broader perspective. Rejecting the seduction, Odysseus embraces the positive aspects of vision. He seeks inner transformation and transcends his former self.

Odysseus survived the Sirens' song by remaining tied to the mast of his ship. Here, on Kalypso's isle, he remains securely tied to his vision of homecoming and reunion with his wife and family. His strong vision keeps him tied to reality.

Those who seek inner transformation are those who are ready for it. Sometimes it may seem that the attainment of a goal must be far, far in the future. If we think we have to wait until our life is nearly over to accomplish a goal, we may view that goal as too distant or too hard to reach. We may postpone our efforts or give up. Acknowledging and celebrating daily victories, not just major milestones, motivates us to keep moving forward and to stay committed to our vision.

If we have a goal that is challenging or has a timeline that extends far into the future, it will test the mettle of our soul to hold firm to it. At times we might feel as though we are walking alone through a long, dark night.

Can we, like Odysseus, hold steady to our cherished dreams for as long as it takes to reach them? Such a test of endurance will require that our higher self rule over our lesser desires. In order to resist temptation, we must first have the ability to recognize it. A clue to identifying inordinate desires is that they deplete our energy and prevent us from fueling our higher desires. Here, holding resolutely to our higher will and vision will prove vital to our success. Endurance, faith, vision and love will keep us moving toward our victory.

LOVE, THE ULTIMATE AND HIGHEST GOAL

In *Man's Search for Meaning*, Dr. Viktor Frankl shared observations forged in his own trial by fire. They are, in effect, keys for getting through a "dark night" no matter where we are in the world or how the test presents itself to us. Three of the keys Frankl named are vision, faith and love. He was in dire, seemingly hopeless circumstances when thoughts of his wife suddenly came to mind. He wrote:

> *My mind clung to my wife's image, imagining it with an uncanny acuteness. I heard her answering me, saw her smile, her frank and encouraging look....*
>
> *A thought transfixed me: for the first time in my life I saw the truth...that love is the ultimate and the highest goal to which man can aspire. Then I grasped the meaning of the greatest secret that human poetry and human thought and belief have to impart: "The salvation of man is through love and in love." I understood how a man who has nothing left in this world*

still may know bliss, be it only for a brief moment, in the contemplation of his beloved. In a position of utter desolation, when man cannot express himself in positive action, when his only achievement may consist in enduring his sufferings in the right way—an honorable way—in such a position man can, through loving contemplation of the image he carries of his beloved, achieve fulfillment.

Frankl said that he sustained his inner strength by keeping a vision of a future goal and visualizing the outcome as if his sufferings were in the past. He wrote:

I kept thinking of the endless little problems of our miserable life.... I became disgusted with the state of affairs which compelled me, daily and hourly, to think of only such trivial things. I forced my thoughts to turn to another subject.

Suddenly I saw myself standing on the platform of a well-lit, warm and pleasant lecture room. In front of me sat an attentive audience on comfortable upholstered seats. I was giving a lecture...! By this method I succeeded somehow in rising above the situation, above the sufferings of the moment, and I observed them as if they were already of the past.[12]

ANCHORING YOUR INSIGHTS

Ten o'Clock Line

TESTS OF VISION

STRENGTHS	WEAKNESSES
keeps vision of life's purpose; prioritizes desires	selfishness, self-love, distorted self-image; loses tie to reality
power to transform and regenerate	self-indulgent, self-destructive
frank, emotionally mature, able to forgive	sarcastic, vindictive, resentful, unforgiving
loyal, compassionate, caring, protective	possessive, jealous, controlling, selfish
endurance, determination to achieve goals	invests power in the wrong purposes
penetrating mind; intuitive; seeks deep meaning	secretive, manipulative

WHO AM I?
TEN O'CLOCK LINE: VISION

Take a moment to think about vision in your life. Reflect on the chart of strengths and weaknesses and use it to evaluate your expressions of vision. Later in this chapter, you will have an opportunity to map your strategy for turning weaknesses into strengths.

What are my greatest strengths in relation to vision?

_____
_____
_____

What are my greatest weaknesses in relation to vision?

_____
_____
_____

Thus far in my life, how have I handled challenges involving the vision of my goal and desires or circumstances that pulled me away from it? Would I handle any of those situations differently now? How?

_____
_____
_____

What can I learn about myself and keeping the vision of my goal from Odysseus' experience?

_____
_____
_____

WINNING STRATEGIES
TEN O'CLOCK LINE: VISION

PUT FIRST THINGS FIRST. Prioritize your desires. How many *things* do we really need in order to be fulfilled and to achieve our goals? Sometimes the things of this world can trip us up. In the course of life we are all tempted in small ways or great. If we look at our activities, how many times do we say we want to reach a goal only to realize a few weeks later that we have totally dropped it? If we have the vision to see through and beyond the temptation, as Odysseus does, then we will hold our vision steady on what really matters to us.

Life presents many opportunities to take the easy way out, to settle for a lesser prize. Know what is important to you, what you value most in yourself, in others and in the world. Know what you want to accomplish and the steps you still need to take to fulfill your dreams. If you know this, you will be far better prepared to recognize temptation and to stay on track.

Envision your goals so strongly that temptation to let go of your dream is not tempting.

BREAK FREE FROM INORDINATE DESIRES. How do you know which desires are ordinate and which are not? Inordinate desires enslave. They may bring a temporary sense of satisfaction but leave you feeling that you are not your own master. They tie up creative energy that you need to fuel your vision and reach your goals.

Once you have identified an inordinate desire, the next step is to make a determination to be free of it. Inordinate desires stem from deeper, unmet needs. But indulging them will not, in fact, meet those needs. When you understand why you do something that is leading you farther away from what you really want in life, you will find it easier to break free.

If you are caught in a trap of inordinate desire, the way out is to look inside to understand your deeper need.

When you are in harmony with your higher self, you will discover better ways to fill your needs that will lead to deep and lasting fulfillment.

CLEARLY COMMUNICATE YOUR NEEDS TO OTHERS. At times we may ignore or hide needs and desires because we are reticent to communicate personal information. We may brood or feel bottled up, as Odysseus brooded daily on Kalypso's shore. Brooding may act as a wall to insulate us against hurt. But we may become frustrated or angry when our needs aren't met.

But if you don't articulate your needs, no one else will know that they exist. Or they may just be more interested in fulfilling their own needs and wants. Communicate your needs and desires.

By your words and actions, you can let others know how to treat you and give them the opportunity to respond in a positive way.

RESOLVE ANY ANGER MASKED AS PASSIVITY. Anger can run deep. It doesn't always manifest as aggression. Sometimes anger masquerades as extreme passivity. Reflecting on issues that have kept you from reaching your goals can help you discover any anger that is hidden beneath the passivity.

Odysseus told Athena that he felt abandoned and forgotten by her. But remember that underneath anger we usually find emotional pain and deep hurt. Unresolved anger can also lead to self-destructive tendencies. If you can discover why you feel hurt, you can deal with it. You can free the energy that has been tied up in these emotions and the situations behind them. If you forgive yourself and others and lock into higher aspects of your being to show you the vision of a better way, you will start to realize a shift.

When you resolve the source of negative emotions, the intense energy stored in them is free to fuel your mission.

KEEP FAITH IN YOUR VISION. To stay afloat during difficult times, we need to cling to our faith in our vision as Odysseus clung to that broken timber on the open sea. When you feel discouraged, you may be tempted to let go of the things that can help you most—for example, staying in touch with a trusted friend, reading uplifting books, communing with your higher self. Building and maintaining a strong support system can help you avoid discouragement and self-indulgence and instead find ways to keep faith in your vision.

During difficult challenges, instead of giving in to your emotions, commune with your higher self to calm your heart. Your higher mind will calm you, assuring you that what you are going through will pass and that you will make it through the dark night.

By cultivating calm faith in your vision, you will be able to continue to fulfill your duties and keep moving toward your goal.

WHERE AM I GOING?
TEN O'CLOCK LINE: VISION

As you reflect on the following questions, you may find it helpful to review the various aspects of vision in the chart on p. 240 and "The Stuff Heroes Are Made Of" on pp. 4–5, as well as the Winning Strategies. Using the questions below, map out a strategy to apply the insights you've gained.

In the tests of vision presented by my current life circumstances, how can I use my strengths constructively?

_____
_____
_____

How can I turn any weakness I may have into an expression of vision that I can claim as a new strength?

_____
_____
_____

Can I take steps to delve into the depths of my being to find the cause and free up more of my creative energy? What are those steps I need to take?

_____
_____
_____

How can I manage my resources more wisely and dedicate more of them to achieving my goals?

_____
_____
_____

MANY PERSONS HAVE A WRONG IDEA OF
WHAT CONSTITUTES TRUE HAPPINESS.
IT IS NOT ATTAINED THROUGH SELF-
GRATIFICATION BUT THROUGH FIDELITY
TO A WORTHY PURPOSE.

HELEN KELLER

BULGARIA

START

Istanbul

Kesan

Komotini

Maronia

Çanakkale

Troy

GREECE

END

TUR

Sparta

Athens

Mycenae

Pylos

Sparta

CRETE

SECURING THE VICTORY

Eleven o'Clock Line

SECURING THE VICTORY

*It's light work for the gods who rule the skies
to exalt a mortal man.*
ODYSSEUS

The Phaiakians have just brought Odysseus home to his native island, Ithaca. They have showered him with gifts amounting to a great treasure. Odysseus is sound asleep when the sailors place him carefully on the sand and pile the gifts under a nearby olive tree. Athena disguises the island, and when he awakens he thinks he is in yet another strange land.

Then Athena, disguised as a young shepherd boy, appears to Odysseus. He asks where he is and she answers, teasingly: "You must be a fool, stranger, or come from no-where, if you really have to ask what land this is. Trust me, it's not so nameless after all.... The name of Ithaca's reached as far as Troy, and Troy, they say, is a long hard sail from Greece." (XIII:237–239, 248–249)

Too crafty to give himself away, Odysseus invents

a long tale describing how he came to this place. Athena drops her disguise, saying: "Whoever gets around you must be sharp and guileful as a snake; even a god might bow to you in ways of dissimulation! You! You chameleon! Bottomless bag of tricks!" (XIII:291–293)

Athena has been testing Odysseus. Would he reveal his identity? Would he make a proud statement about being a king returned? Would he betray his emotion on coming home? Not Odysseus. His cautious and ingenious replies win Athena's high praise.

Athena helps Odysseus to stow his treasures in the recesses of a deep cave, then covers the opening with a stone. Then she describes what is happening in his palace, where one hundred and eight suitors have been trying to win the hand of his wife, Penelope, in order to gain control of the kingdom.

Athena tells Odysseus: "Three long years they have played master in your house: three years trying to win your lovely lady, making gifts as though betrothed." The suitors have helped themselves to Odysseus' best fattened animals and provisions and have drained his vats of vintage wines, feasting every night at his expense. Penelope, meanwhile, does all she can to hold off the suitors. Though Penelope is "forever grieving," her thoughts and her heart remained fixed on Odysseus; she still hopes for his return. (XIII:377–379)

After hearing about the arrogant intruders, Odysseus cries out: "O grey-eyed one, fire my heart and brace me! I'll take on fighting men three hundred strong if you fight at my back, immortal lady!" (XIII:389–391) Athena promises to be with Odysseus but says that for his own

*Athena tips her golden wand and the beggar
turns into Lord Odysseus. His son is thunder-
struck.*

safety he must be disguised until the battle is over. She
transforms him into an old ugly beggar dressed in vile rags.
Odysseus accepts this transformation without a word; he
trusts Athena completely.

Next, Athena sends Odysseus to the home of a
swineherd who has remained loyal to him all these years. In
the swineherd's hut, Odysseus learns all that has happened
on Ithaca since he left for Troy. When the time is right,
Athena reveals Odysseus to his son, Telemachos. They
begin to plan together how they will regain the kingdom.

The suitors, watching the old beggar with the bow, taunt him, saying, "Dealer in old bows!" and "Maybe he has one like it at home!"

Telemachos goes ahead to the palace and then, at the appointed time, Odysseus makes his way there. He continues to play the part of the beggar, begging food from the suitors who sit feasting at his own well-supplied table. Odysseus suffers the taunts and insults of the suitors. He does not even reveal his identity to his wife, Penelope.

Athena further instructs Odysseus and his son in their battle plan. One night after the suitors depart for their homes, Odysseus and Telemachos remove Odysseus' store of weapons from the great room, where the suitors feast every day, into a vaulted storeroom. As they work, Athena holds up a "lamp of purest light." Telemachos cries out in amazement: "All around I see the walls and roof beams, pedestals and pillars, lighted as though by white fire blazing near. One of the gods of heaven is in this place!" (XIX:34–40)

Penelope, counseled in subtle ways by Athena, knows that something is afoot and she feels uneasy. Late that night, Penelope speaks privately and at length with the beggar (Odysseus in disguise), seeking any news of Odysseus. At the conclusion of their talk, she tells the beggar of the bow contest she has devised for the suitors. She explains to him that Odysseus, in his time, would take twelve axe heads and "line them up, all twelve, at intervals like a ship's ribbing; then he'd back away a long way off and whip an arrow through." (XIX:573–575) She tells the beggar she will marry the suitor who can shoot through all twelve axes. Odysseus encourages her not to delay.

The next day Penelope enters the great hall and announces her challenge:

> *My lords, hear me: suitors indeed, you commandeered this house to feast and drink in, day and night, my husband being long gone, long out of mind. You found no justification for yourselves—none except your lust to marry me. Stand up, then: we now declare a contest for that prize. Here is my lord Odysseus' hunting bow. Bend and string it if you can. Who sends an arrow through iron axe-helve sockets, twelve in line? I join my life with his.* (XXI:68–77)

None of the arrogant suitors can even bend the bow. Still in disguise, Odysseus asks to be given a turn with the bow. Among taunts and raucous objections from the suitors, Telemachos commands that the beggar be given a turn. Odysseus' loyal swineherd takes the bow from the suitors and passes it to the beggar. Odysseus takes his time, "turning the bow, tapping it, every inch, for borings that termites might have made." (XXI:393–395) This makes the suitors ridicule him even more. Then, effortlessly, with one motion, Odysseus strings the bow. He plucks the string to test its pitch.

Suddenly the hall becomes hushed. The suitors' faces change. Zeus sends one loud crack of thunder. Odysseus picks one arrow, nocks it, and draws the bowstring back. The arrow flashes "clean as a whistle through every socket ring" and grazes not one. (XXI:422–423)

The fight is on. Odysseus drops his disguise and proceeds, with the help of his son and two loyal servants, to kill every suitor. Athena helps by spoiling all the suitors' shots. She also arranges for Penelope to fall asleep upstairs, so that Penelope will not be awakened by the battle.

After the battle is over, Odysseus commands the unfaithful servants to remove the dead bodies and clean the great room. Next he commands that the treacherous servants be taken to the courtyard and killed. After the work is done, Odysseus calls for "brimstone and a brazier —medicinal fumes." (XXII:480–481) With the cleansing fumes of sulfur, Odysseus purifies his palace.

When order is restored in the palace, Odysseus' faithful old nurse runs upstairs to awaken Penelope. "Wake, wake up, dear child! Penelope, come down, see with your own eyes what all these years you longed for! Odysseus is here!... And he has killed your suitors." Penelope replies: "Dear nurse, the gods have touched you. They can put chaos into the clearest head." (XXIII:5–8, 11–14)

The nurse tries to convince Penelope, but Penelope hesitates to believe that the love of her life has really returned. When she enters the hall, she sits in the firelight across the room from Odysseus, who is still disguised as the old beggar, covered with blood, his clothes in tatters. She remains silent, unable to look directly into his face.

Odysseus goes to be bathed. He returns to the hall dressed in fine clothing. Athena suffuses him with beauty. He reproaches his wife for her stubborn heart. Then he tells the nurse to make up a bed for him. Penelope shows herself to be the perfect match for Odysseus. She tells the nurse to bring Odysseus' bed out into the hall, thereby cleverly testing him to reveal a secret that only he would know. He exclaims that he fashioned their bed out of a living olive tree that remained rooted in the earth. Only then does she run to embrace him.

Then Athena "held back the night, and night lingered long at the western edge of the earth, while in the east she reined in Dawn of the golden throne at Ocean's banks." (XXIII:243–244) During the long night, Odysseus and Penelope share their stories with each other and the reunited pair have their fill of love and sleep.

THE VALUE OF A MENTOR

The relationship between Athena and Odysseus is special and touching. It is unique in all of ancient Greek literature for its intimacy. Odysseus complains that Athena abandoned him after Troy. But she affirms: "I...am always with you in times of trial, a shield to you in battle.... For my part, never had I despaired; I felt sure of your coming home, though all your men should perish; but I never cared to fight Poseidon, Father's brother, in his baleful rage with you for taking his son's eye." (XIII:300–301, 339–343)

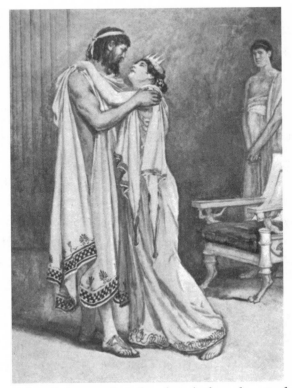

After Odysseus describes their bed made out of a living olive tree, Penelope, with eyes brimming tears, runs to him and throws her arms around his neck.

In other words, he had to make amends on his own for blinding the Cyclops. She would not interfere. The same is true for us. We may receive a tremendous amount of help and encouragement from our teachers, mentors and others, and these can and will help. But we have to balance our accounts on our own.

In this episode, Athena helps Odysseus in all sorts of ways. She arranges the strategy for the battle. She lights up the dark hall. She comforts him when he lays awake the night before the battle, wondering how he can win against more than a hundred men. She comes to him and says: "What am I? Your goddess-guardian to the end in all your trials. Now you, too, go to sleep.... You'll come out soon enough on the other side of trouble." (XX:47–48, 52–53)

What a prophecy! At last, Odysseus, the man who has for so long brought trouble to himself and others, will be freed from his burdens. Yet even while she saves him, Athena keeps on testing her protégé. She continually incites the suitors to taunt him to see how he will react. He is not provoked. He keeps his battle plan and his vision of victory firmly in mind, and he passes his tests.

In the thick of the battle, Athena waits before she enters the scene. First, Homer reminds us, "father and son must prove their mettle." (XXII:237–238) But when all the suitors turn on Odysseus at once, Athena saves the day by misdirecting their arrows.

NEVER TAKE VICTORY FOR GRANTED

In this final trial, Odysseus demonstrates that he has learned a great deal about himself. Working hand in hand with Athena and joining forces with his son and loyal servants, Odysseus deftly conquers his enemies.

The goddess Athena symbolizes Odysseus' higher self, upon which his victory depends. Throughout this trial, Odysseus follows Athena's instructions to a tee. He stays practical and focused on executing his strategies. In tune with his higher self, he overcomes the suitors.

The suitors represent the negative traits Odysseus has encountered and been tested on throughout his voyage. Some of these traits nearly undid him in earlier trials; in this trial he proves his mastery over them all. The qualities he has developed and strengthened during his voyage now serve him well and see him through to his victory.

As Odysseus' story shows, we can never take victory for granted. To secure the victory, we must first do the inner work. This is the profound understanding we gain from the trials of Odysseus: When the inner work is done, the outer work goes smoothly.

In the episode with Aiolos and the bag of winds, Odysseus failed to communicate essential information to his team, and the cost for all of them was high. Now he communicates essential information to his son and loyal servants and the teamwork goes without a hitch.

In previous episodes, Odysseus suffered the harmful consequences of being reckless and revealing his identity too soon. In this episode, he demonstrates self-control by keeping his temper and ego in check. No longer self-righteous and boastful, as he was with the Cyclops, he now uses restraint and good judgment, thereby showing wife and son, suitors and servants that he has earned the right to be king. Only then does he claim it.

SELF-RESTRAINT, PATIENCE AND HUMILITY

Throughout this final episode, Odysseus' timing is precise. He shows self-restraint, patience and humility—factors essential to his victory. Earlier in his journey, Odysseus was at times reckless, impatient and boastful. But in his interactions with the suitors, it is they who embody the negative qualities. Odysseus shows great self-control.

Self-Restraint. The suitors are tactless and quarrelsome and they use sharp speech with Odysseus. They laugh at him, an affront not taken lightly in those days. On the island of the Phaiakians, a young man had taunted Odysseus to force his participation in an athletic contest. Reacting angrily, Odysseus had immediately proved himself more than equal to the challenge; he had felt compelled to defend his sense of honor.

In great contrast, when the suitors treat Odysseus roughly and throw things at him, he does not react. Keeping his strategy and goal foremost in his mind, he responds with self-restraint and patience. If Odysseus had acted rashly and retaliated, he would have lost everything, because it was not yet the time to attack or to reveal himself. Instead, he patiently bides his time.

Patience. Soon after Odysseus' arrival at Ithaca, Athena had spelled out his test: "Patience, iron patience, you must show; so give it out to neither man nor woman that you are back from wandering. Be silent under all injuries, even blows from men." (XIII:307–310)

After the suitors are slain, Odysseus says that they met their death because they were disrespectful and reckless. Symbolically, he triumphs because he has overcome these character flaws. He has done his homework. To repeat a key point, when the inner work is done, the outer work goes smoothly. Because Odysseus prepared himself, everything goes smoothly and the events unfold like clockwork. However, he still does not take anything for granted. Although Athena had assured him that his troubles would soon be over, he is neither overconfident nor reckless.

Patience is one of Odysseus' virtues as well as Penelope's. Penelope, the loyal wife, waits for her husband for twenty years. At one point when the suitors press her to choose one of them, she successfully holds them off by saying that before she can marry she must weave a shroud for her aging father-in-law. Every day she weaves on her great loom, and every night she undoes her weaving and starts all over again the next day. After three years of this, an unfaithful servant exposes her ploy and the suitors discover her deception. She must then finish her weaving. She continues to hold the suitors at bay by telling them she must wait until her son is grown up before she can remarry.

Humility. Another factor in Odysseus' success is his humility, forged in the fiery crucible of his voyage. His pride is put to the test when Athena disguises him as a lowly beggar. When the suitors taunt him, he maintains a demeanor appropriate to his disguise. Had he reacted with rage or indignation, he would have jeopardized the success of the battle plan.

After the slaughter, Odysseus' old nurse surveys the scene and raises her head "to cry over his triumph." He grasps her, checking her cry, and upbraids her: "Rejoice inwardly. No crowing aloud, old woman. To glory over slain men is no piety. Destiny and the gods' will vanquished these, and their own hardness. They respected no one, good or bad, who came their way. For this, and folly, a bad end befell them." (XXII:408, 411–417)

Odysseus sees himself as an instrument for the will of the gods and for divine retribution. He remains humble, refusing to gloat over the dead suitors, and literally grows in stature. Homer describes Odysseus' appearance after the battle and following his bath. "Athena lent him beauty, head to foot. She made him taller, and massive, too, with crisping hair in curls." (XXIII:156–158)

DRAWING THE BOW OF MASTERY

To pass this final trial, Odysseus had to internalize the lessons and archetypal qualities of all the preceding trials. If he had not done so, his final performance would not have gone as smoothly and his resounding victory might instead have ended as an unfulfilled dream.

Homer could not have picked a more splendid device to show Odysseus' mastery than the bow. To shoot a bow with accuracy takes farsightedness and an exact aim. If the archer's aim is too far to the right or the left, he will miss his mark. Odysseus strings his bow with ease and his aim is precise. His arrow flies cleanly through all twelve axe sockets. This signifies his culminating mastery of all twelve trials. Odysseus no longer indulges in extremes.

The heirloom hunting bow Odysseus uses in this episode originally belonged to the Greek god Apollo, the archer god who stands for authority, law and order, and moderation—virtues Odysseus exemplifies in this episode. The day on which Odysseus slew the suitors was a festival day of Apollo.

AN UNSHAKABLE
FOUNDATION OF WHOLENESS

This final episode is a story of contrasts. It contrasts the former Odysseus with the mature Odysseus. The outer challenge Odysseus faces in this trial is to regain his wife and his kingdom by casting out the arrogant suitors. His inner challenge is to put his internal house in order by purging himself of unruly passions and desires. In a superb display of mastery, Odysseus shows that he has truly cultivated the qualities of a hero and has mastered the traits that could have spelled his defeat.

Odysseus' faithful and wise wife, Penelope, represents Odysseus' soul. By conquering his inner foes, represented by the suitors, Odysseus frees his soul.

Odysseus and Penelope's bed, made from an olive tree that is still rooted in the earth, symbolizes the strong and unshakeable foundation of their love. The rooted tree trunk is also a sign of stability and oneness. As the symbol of the goddess Athena, the olive tree represents the blessing of their union by Athena.

Earlier, Odysseus says that "the best thing in the world" is "a strong house held in serenity where man and wife agree. Woe to their enemies, joy to their friends!" (VI:182–185) Here, symbolically, he is praising the ideal of *wholeness*, a spiritual state in which the male and female elements within a person are in complete harmony. He is saying that the best thing in the world is the strength that comes from inner serenity and inner harmony.

A person who has attained inner peace cannot be conquered.

❂ ANCHORING YOUR INSIGHTS ☩

Eleven o'Clock Line

TESTS OF VICTORY

STRENGTHS	WEAKNESSES
patience, self-restraint, moderation	irritable, impatient, reactive, revengeful, reckless
plans wisely, practical, dependable to the end	lacks focus; lost in abstractions and theory, changeable
frank, straight-forward, truthful	tactless, cynical, quarrelsome, sharp in speech
self-confident but humble	self-righteous, exaggerating or boastful
high-minded, idealistic, insightful	fanatical, small-minded, narrow-minded
just, loyal, ethical; uses good judgment	disrespectful, irresponsible, intolerant of restrictions

WHO AM I?
ELEVEN O'CLOCK LINE: VICTORY

Take a moment to think about victory in your life. Reflect on the chart of strengths and weaknesses and use it to evaluate your expressions of victory. Later in this chapter, you will have an opportunity to map your strategy for turning weaknesses into strengths.

What are my greatest strengths in relation to victory?

_____

_____

What are my greatest weaknesses in relation to victory? What dropped stitches might I have that could possibly prevent my victory achieving my goals in life?

_____

_____

_____

Thus far in my life, how have I handled challenges involving aspects of victory? Would I handle any of those situations differently now? How?

_____

_____

_____

What can I learn about myself and the importance of self-restraint, patience and humility to my victory from Odysseus' experience?

_____

_____

_____

WINNING STRATEGIES
ELEVEN O'CLOCK LINE: VICTORY

TAKE ACTION TO HEAL AND FREE YOUR SOUL.
We must all free our own soul by working through the things in our being and life that we must contend with so that no one can take our wholeness from us. Wholeness is what we are striving for. When we do not have wholeness, we suffer. Recall Odysseus' suffering on Kalypso's island; in the absence of wholeness he felt great emotional pain.

Until you have achieved wholeness, you can be ever so grateful that you *can* feel your soul's longing and pain, because through feeling it you become aware of your opportunity to take action to heal the wounded parts of your being and thereby attain greater wholeness.

Create an unshakeable foundation of wholeness that will take you to your victory.

RESIST THE TEMPTATION OF RESENTMENT AND RETALIATION. Especially when we are tired and have been under great pressure or burdens in our life, it's easy to over-react in resentment to perceived or actual injustices and injuries. Athena warns Odysseus not to react when the suitors try to provoke him; if he does, he will lose everything.

Emotions are more difficult to control when we are off balance. Sometimes this can be from irregular eating and sleeping habits. Discipline yourself or have a friend or family member remind you to take care of yourself so that you are not emotionally vulnerable or volatile, especially when you are working or studying long hours.

The challenge may also be unexpected, right when victory is in sight. Say, for instance, that someone approaches you in a rage or accuses you falsely. What do you do? You can say you must excuse yourself and will be back shortly. Count to ten. Take a walk and draw slow, deep breaths.

Remember that your goal is more important than any emotional outburst.

CULTIVATE HUMILITY. Although his trials were brutal, Odysseus certainly has much to boast of when he returns to Ithaca. But his pride has become tempered with wisdom and humility. He knows he would not have made it home without the intercession of the gods. When we are centered in our higher self, we are humbly grateful for every victory, grateful for those who taught us and helped us, grateful for the talents we have been given.

If you have worked through and mastered many things, as Odysseus has, you can still be susceptible to pride, especially subtle pride. This is when it is more important than ever to cultivate humility and patiently wait for the natural timing of the victory that is yours.

Your higher self has petals that are unfolding in the rose of your being—don't force the bloom.

NEVER TAKE YOUR VICTORY FOR GRANTED. Sometimes people have worked hard and just before the finish line they overlook seemingly minor details that can result in their project failing or a deal falling through. Odysseus embodies the attribute of big-picture thinking but also pays careful attention to every detail.

Be mindful of details rather than rushing the finish line. This is the point at which everything that you have learned and mastered can be brought to bear upon the last challenges standing between you and your victory.

We can never take our victories for granted. In the eleventh hour, it is important not to be overly optimistic, but to be prepared and stay alert.

TRANSLATE YOUR IDEAS INTO ACTION IN A PRACTICAL WAY. When you are working to achieve a goal, be sure not only to pay attention to the details but also to create a practical overall plan. Get opinions from others and consider carefully before moving into action. Try not to act impulsively or have your head in the clouds with ideas and theories. If you are working with a group, be dependable and diligently follow through with what you have agreed upon.

Victory is envisioned in your mind and heart and then carried out as physical reality.

WHERE AM I GOING?
ELEVEN O'CLOCK LINE: VICTORY

As you reflect on the following questions, you may find it helpful to review the various aspects of victory in the chart on p. 265 and "The Stuff Heroes Are Made Of" on pp. 4–5, as well as the Winning Strategies. Using the questions below, map out a strategy to apply the insights you've gained.

In the tests of victory presented by my current life circumstances, how can I use my strengths constructively?

_____

_____

How can I turn any weakness I may have into an expression of victory that I can claim as a new strength?

_____

_____

_____

What are the most important steps I can take to prepare myself to draw the bow of my mastery and aim for a major goal?

_____

_____

_____

In what ways can I pass on what I have learned through my tests and trials to others? How can I share my sense of victory?

_____

_____

_____

EVERY GREAT ACHIEVEMENT IS THE
VICTORY OF A FLAMING HEART.

RALPH WALDO EMERSON

Conclusion

THE CALL TO ADVENTURE

The End Is Just a
New Beginning

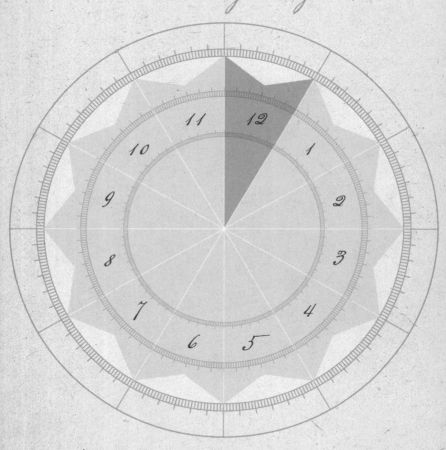

THE CALL
TO ADVENTURE

*The only true voyage of discovery...
is not in visiting new lands
but in having other eyes.*
ODYSSEUS

By the time Odysseus reaches his home in Ithaca, he has been stripped of many elements of his lesser self. He functions in tune with his higher self and in sync with his mentor, Athena. On his homeward journey, Odysseus failed some tests and passed others. Through it all he learned the lessons he needed to learn to attain a greater level of wholeness. He has become a wiser soul, a better man.

When Odysseus and Penelope reunite, Odysseus tells her, "Dear wife, we have not yet come to the limit of all our trials. There is unmeasured labor left for the future, both difficult and great, and all of it I must accomplish. So the soul of Teiresias prophesied to me." (XXIII:248–251) Odysseus must undertake a journey to make amends to Poseidon. Once he has accomplished this, the prophet

276 OF YOUR SOUL

said, he will live in peace and prosperity unto old age. Penelope replies, "Then there is hope that you shall have an escape from your troubles." (XXIII:287)

MOVING EVER HIGHER

With this bittersweet scene, Homer alludes to the unending nature of the soul's odyssey. The English poet Alfred, Lord Tennyson captured the eternal call to adventure in his poem *Ulysses*. (Odysseus is known in Roman mythology as Ulysses.) In this poem Tennyson depicts the hero as aspiring to move ever higher. He speaks of how dull and unrewarding it is to stand still. Even though we have passed through many experiences already, there is always another noble work to be done:

> I cannot rest from travel; I will drink
> Life to the lees. All times I have enjoyed
> Greatly, have suffered greatly, both with those
> That loved me, and alone....
> I am a part of all that I have met....
> How dull it is to pause, to make an end,
> To rust unburnished, not to shine in use!
> As though to breathe were life!...
> Old age hath yet his honor and his toil.
> Death closes all; but something ere the end,
> Some work of noble note, may yet be done....
> The lights begin to twinkle from the rocks;
> The long day wanes; the slow moon climbs; the deep
> Moans round with many voices. Come, my friends,
> 'Tis not too late to seek a newer world.
> Push off, and sitting well in order smite

The sounding furrows; for my purpose holds
To sail beyond the sunset, and the baths
Of all the western stars, until I die.
It may be that the gulfs will wash us down;
It may be we shall touch the Happy Isles,
And see the great Achilles, whom we knew.
Though much is taken, much abides; and though
We are not now that strength which in old days
Moved earth and heaven, that which we are, we are,
One equal temper of heroic hearts,
Made weak by time and fate, but strong in will
To strive, to seek, to find, and not to yield.[13]

HEROES AND HEROINES

Odysseus' adventures are the adventures of every soul. Thus, we can take heart for our own voyage of self-discovery and see our whole life as a sacred adventure. We need not ever be satisfied with our current lot, with our current level of mastery. There will always be more to conquer— more seas to cross, more mountains to climb. If we meet the challenge, we will keep on moving, keep on adventuring in the odyssey of our soul.

If we remain steadfast, we will reach resting places in our journey. But the adventures never really end; they continue cycle upon cycle. Odysseus will begin his next adventure with access to all the qualities and traits he has mastered and integrated in his just-completed odyssey. In the future, as he undergoes more soul testing, he will spiral even higher.

The *Odyssey* is rich with inner meaning. The experience of Odysseus shows that mistakes and suffering are a part of life. They are our teachers, and through embracing their lessons we grow wiser and more self-aware. As you work with the inner trials of Odysseus as they relate to your own, you will continue to discover more about yourself.

We have reached the end of our journey with Odysseus. In keeping with the tradition in Odysseus' day to offer parting gifts to guests, we offer you a set of keys and a map for your own continuing odyssey.

KEYS TO VICTORY

1. Keep your eye on your goal.
2. Don't be afraid to make a mistake.
3. Courageously accept and face your trials.
4. When you make a mistake, bounce back.
5. Learn from your mistakes.
6. Don't be afraid of pain and suffering.
7. Endure.
8. Be open to discovering more about your inner self.
9. Don't dwell on the past.
10. Respect the divine in whatever form that takes for you.
11. Be obedient to your inner guidance.
12. Have a mentor, teacher or guide who intercedes for you and holds a vision of your destiny fulfilled.

Map of My Inner Self

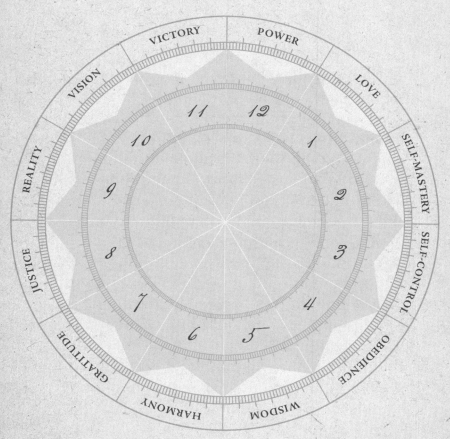

YOUR VISION WILL BECOME CLEAR
ONLY WHEN YOU LOOK INTO YOUR HEART.....
WHO LOOKS OUTSIDE, DREAMS.
WHO LOOKS INSIDE, AWAKENS.

C. G. JUNG